# ABUNDANT TRUTH INTERNATIONAL MINISTRIES

Ministry Guides Series

# The Believer's Guide to the Apostolic Ministry

A Comprehensive Study of the Apostolic Ministry in the Church

Roderick Levi Evans

## The Believer's Guide to the Apostolic Ministry
*A Comprehensive Study of the Apostolic Ministry in the Church*

All Rights Reserved ©2014 by Roderick L. Evans

*No part of this book may be reproduced or transmitted in any form or by any means, graphic, electronic, or mechanical, including photocopying, recording, taping, or by any information storage or retrieval system, without the permission in writing from the publisher.*

Front & Back Cover Designs by Abundant Truth Publishing

Abundant Truth Publishing
an imprint of Abundant Truth International Ministries
For information address:
Abundant Truth International
P.O. Box 126
Camden, NC 27921

Unless otherwise indicated, all of the scripture quotations are taken from the *Authorized King James Version* of the Bible. Scripture quotations marked with NIV are taken from the *New International Version* of the Bible. Scripture quotations marked with NASV are taken from the *New American Standard Version* of the Bible. Scripture quotations marked with Amplified are taken from the *Amplified Bible*.

ISBN: 978-1-60141-597-4

Printed in the United States of America

# Contents

Introduction

**Book 1 – The Making of the Apostle**　　　1
Introduction　　　3

**Chapter 1- Marring of the Apostle**　　　7
Pride　　　10
Suffering　　　11
Embarrassment　　　12

**Chapter 2 - Love of the Apostle**　　　15
The Love of the Apostle　　　17
The Word and the Apostle　　　19
The Endearing Love　　　20

**Chapter 3 - Building of the Apostle**　　　25
Spiritual Consecration　　　26
Spiritual Understanding　　　27
Spiritual Insight　　　27
Spiritual Motivation　　　28
Spiritual Speech　　　29
Spiritual Responsibility　　　29
Spiritual Doctrine　　　30
Spiritual Reflection　　　31

# Contents (cont.)

| | |
|---|---|
| **Chapter 4 - The Apostle's Character** | **33** |
| The Attitude of the Sprit | 36 |
| The Empathy of the Spirit | 39 |
| The Endurance of the Spirit | 42 |
| | |
| **Book 2 - The Apostle Question** | **45** |
| Preface | 47 |
| Introduction | 49 |
| | |
| **Chapter 1 – What is an Apostle?** | **55** |
| Apostolic Ministry in the Old Testament | 58 |
| Apostolic Ministry in the New Testament | 64 |
| | |
| **Chapter 2 – The Call of an Apostle** | **73** |
| Acknowledging the Apostolic Call | 75 |
| Answering the Apostolic Call | 82 |
| Accepting the Apostolic Call | 88 |
| | |
| **Chapter 3 – The Office of the Apostle** | **93** |
| *Nine Functions of the Apostle* | *95* |
| *Focus of Apostles* | *102* |

# Contents (cont.)

**Chapter 4 – The Roles of the Apostle**     **105**

Apostles as Ambassadors     107

*Apostles as Fathers*     *114*

**Chapter 5 – Apostles in Perspective**     **123**

Apostles and the Church     125

Apostles and Pastors     132

Apostles versus Prophets     134

Responding to Misconceptions     137

**Chapter 6 – What is Apostleship?**     **151**

The Apostolic Gift     156

The Apostolic Spirit     158

Guidelines for Judging the Apostolic     166

**Chapter 7 – False Apostles**     **171**

Recognizing False Ministers     175

Recognizing False Apostles     179

# Contents (cont.)

**Book 3 - The Apostolic Revolution**    **187**
Preface    189
Introduction    191

**Chapter 1 – The Apostolic Restoration**    **197**
The Ancestral Demonstrations    199
The Apostolic Restored    203

**Chapter 2 - The Apostolic Representative**    **207**
Obedience    211
Love    212
Authentic Apostolic Ministry    215

**Chapter 3 - The Apostolic Refused**    **219**
Judas' Beliefs    222
Judas' Betrayal    225

**Chapter 4 - The Apostolic Rejected**    **233**
Judas' Bleak End    235
The Case for Rejection    239

**Chapter 5 - The Apostolic Respected**    **243**
Peter's Insight    246

# Contents (cont.)

| | |
|---|---|
| Peter's Integrity | 248 |
| Peter's Invocation | 250 |

## Book 4 – The Apostolic Paradigm Shift — 253
| | |
|---|---|
| Preface | 255 |
| Introduction | 257 |

### Chapter 1 – The Apostolic Paradigm Shift — 259
| | |
|---|---|
| Matthias: The Chosen Apostle | 263 |
| Matthias: The Silent Apostle | 264 |
| Matthias: The Processed Apostle | 266 |
| Matthias: The Prepared Apostle | 267 |
| Matthias: The Committed Apostle | 270 |
| Matthias: The Seer- Apostle | 272 |

### Chapter 2 – The Apostolic Representation — 276
| | |
|---|---|
| Joseph: The Called Apostolic | 278 |
| Joseph: The Secret Apostolic | 280 |
| Joseph: The Processed Apostolic | 281 |
| Joseph: The Prepared Apostolic | 283 |
| Joseph: The Committed Apostolic | 285 |

# Contents (cont.)

**Chapter 3 - The Apostolic Expression** — 291
The Great Outpouring — 293
The Great Revelation — 295

**Chapter 4 - The Apostolic Administration4** — 297
The Great Testimony — 299
The Great Commission — 300

**Chapter 5 – The Apostolic Reformation** — 307
Reformation of Love — 310
Reformation of the Miraculous — 311
Reformation of Disciples — 311

**Book 5 – The Constructing of the Apostolic Person** — 315
Introduction — 317

**Prologue – Understanding Anointings** — 321
Anointings in the Old Testament — 324
Anointings in the New Testament — 328
Office versus Anointing — 333

# Contents (cont.)

| | |
|---|---|
| **Chapter 1- Apostolic Person is a Disciple** | **337** |
| Disciples of the Word | 339 |
| Disciples of the Loyalty | 339 |
| Disciples of Discipline | 340 |
| Disciples of Christ's Example | 340 |
| Disciples Respect Authority | 340 |
| | |
| **Chapter 2 - Apostolic Person is a Son (or Daughter)** | **343** |
| Obedient | 345 |
| Reflect | 345 |
| Follow Example | 346 |
| | |
| **Chapter 3 - The Apostolic Person is a Brother (or Sister)** | **349** |
| Protect | 351 |
| Godly Directives | 351 |
| Trustworthy | 352 |
| | |
| **Chapter 4 – The Apostolic Person's Character** | **353** |
| Foundation of Love | 355 |
| Foundation of Faithfulness | 356 |
| Foundation of Edification | 356 |

# Contents (cont.)

Foundation of Community     357

**Chapter 5 – Recognizing the Apostolic Person**     359
Understanding of the Word     361
Understanding of Impartation     362
Understanding Development     362
Understanding Evangelism     363
Understanding Order     364
Understanding Discernment     365
Understanding Spiritual Gifts     366

**Chapter 6 - Flourishing as an Apostolic Person**     369
Flourish in Study     371
Flourish in Prayer     372
Flourish in Submission     375

# Introduction

Ministry and service are gifts from God. The ministries are multifaceted and sometimes complex. The Ministry Guides Series is designed to offer information that will strengthen, enlighten, and encourage those involved in Christian ministry.

**In this publication**

In this book, we will bring clarity to the roles of apostles, functionality of apostolic ministry, and the apostolic expressions of the apostolic gift. This study is comprised of 5 distinct works on the apostolic office and gift:

1) The Making of the Apostle: The Preparation of the Apostle and Apostolic Minister for Ministry and Service

2) The Apostle Question: Exploring the Role of Apostles in the New Testament Church

3) The Apostolic Revolution: Exploring the Apostolic Restoration and Reformation

4) The Apostolic Paradigm Shift: Examining the Coming Reformation of Apostles and Apostolic Ministry

5) The Constructing of the Apostolic Person : The Preparation of the Apostolic Person for Ministry and Service

It is our prayer that a greater understanding and appreciation for the apostolic gift and ministry will be achieved.

**THE BELIEVER'S GUIDE TO THE APOSTOLIC MINISTRY**

A Comprehensive Study of the Apostolic Ministry in the Church

# -Book 1-
# The Making of the Apostle:
## The Preparation of the Apostle and Apostolic Minister for Ministry and Service

**THE BELIEVER'S GUIDE TO THE APOSTOLIC MINISTRY** — A Comprehensive Study of the Apostolic Ministry in the Church

The training of an apostle is oftentimes humiliating. God will allow disruption in every area of his life to prepare him for service. Those called to the apostolic office should understand that preparation for ministry is in the development of Christ's character. If this is done, the apostle will never come behind in any spiritual gift during ministry. In this book, we will discuss how God builds the apostle for ministry.

# Introduction

Ministry and service in the kingdom of God is a privilege. God calls every member of the Body of Christ to serve for the benefit and welfare of the Body of Christ. However, we must remember that there are personal preparations that God requires for service.

The Potter's Wheel Study Series is designed to help believers recognize and apply the personal preparation that God implements for those called to minister and to serve. It is our prayer that the minister and the laymen will respond to God's personal preparations for ministry and service.

**THE BELIEVER'S GUIDE TO THE APOSTOLIC MINISTRY**  A Comprehensive Study of the Apostolic Ministry in the Church

**THE BELIEVER'S GUIDE TO THE APOSTOLIC MINISTRY** — A Comprehensive Study of the Apostolic Ministry in the Church

In this Publication

The apostle's ministry comes with authority, power, and the miraculous. This is only a part of the apostle's ministry. His ministry serves as a reflection of Christ's ministry to the Church. Consequently, the apostle's character must be solid. Therefore, God will take the apostles through tests, trials, and temptations in order to prepare them for ministry.

The training of an apostle is oftentimes humiliating. God will allow disruption in every area of his life to prepare him for service. Those called to the apostolic office should understand that preparation for ministry is in the development of Christ's character. If this is done, the apostle will never come behind in any spiritual gift during ministry. In this book, we will discuss how God builds the apostle for ministry.

**THE BELIEVER'S GUIDE TO THE APOSTOLIC MINISTRY** — A Comprehensive Study of the Apostolic Ministry in the Church

**THE BELIEVER'S GUIDE TO THE APOSTOLIC MINISTRY** — A Comprehensive Study of the Apostolic Ministry in the Church

-Chapter 1-

# Marring of the Apostle

## Jeremiah's girdle

Jeremiah prophesied to Judah during a time of great rebellion and sin against God. To express His judgment upon Judah, God instructed Jeremiah to hide his girdle in a rock and leave it for a length of time.

*And the word of the Lord came unto me the second time, saying, Take the girdle that thou hast got, which is upon thy loins, and arise, go to Euphrates, and hide it there in a hole of the rock. So I went, and hid it by Euphrates, as the Lord commanded me. And it came to pass after many days, that the Lord said unto me, Arise, go to Euphrates, and take the girdle from thence, which I commanded thee to hide there. Then I went to Euphrates, and digged, and took the girdle from the place where I had hid it: and, behold, the girdle was marred, it was profitable for nothing. (Jeremiah 13:3-7)*

Jeremiah's girdle was marred. When something is marred, it is ruined. Jeremiah's girdle had decayed.

**Pride**

In the following verses, God said that He would mar Jerusalem and Judah's pride. This is what the Lord does to the apostle. **An apostle has to recognize that he is nothing without God.**

Therefore, God will allow the apostle to experience embarrassment and humiliation to prepare him for the authority that is before him. Without understanding his position before God, the apostle will fall into pride and arrogance. Thus, God breaks him down in order to preserve him.

*I am become a fool in glorying; ye have compelled me: for I ought to have been*

> *commended of you: for in nothing am I behind the very chiefest apostles, though I be nothing. (2 Corinthians 12:11)*

Paul spoke of his ministry, but declared he was nothing. Because of God's discipline and training, Paul walked in humility even after years of powerful ministry.

**Suffering**

Apostles will suffer greatly before and during ministry. God allows a continual marring process in their lives to keep them humble and broken before him.

> *For I think that God hath set forth us the apostles last, as it were appointed to death: for we are made a spectacle unto the world, and to angels, and to men. (I Corinthians 4:9)*

Because of the Lord's process, Paul stated

that he felt as if apostles were appointed unto death. This means that the apostle will meet consistent opposition and tests.

Those called to the apostolic office will have testimonies of great rejection, times of poverty, and sickness. They will be the subject of gossip, debate, and slander.

**Embarrassment**

Apostles usually experience embarrassing situations to produce selflessness and humility. These things will happen even after they enter into ministry. There is a consistent call to self-death laid on the apostle. His pride will consistently be marred so that Christ and the Church may shine.

*We are fools for Christ's sake, but ye are wise in Christ; we are weak, but ye are strong; ye are honourable, but we are despised. (I Corinthians 4:10)*

The apostle's self-death results in a fruitful ministry and healthy Church.

*Verily, verily, I say unto you, Except a corn of wheat fall into the ground and die, it abideth alone: but if it die, it bringeth forth much fruit. (John 12:24)*

**THE BELIEVER'S GUIDE TO THE APOSTOLIC MINISTRY**  A Comprehensive Study of the Apostolic Ministry in the Church

-Chapter 2-

# Love of the Apostle:

## Husbands and Wives

Part of the apostle's making is in the area of love. God places a deep love in the apostle for Christ and the Church. *If the apostle's love does not mirror Christ's, he will wreak havoc in the Church. He will damage God's people.* Since apostles stand in Christ's stead, it is important to understand that the Christ-Church relationship is marriage.

As Christ is married to the Church, so are the apostles. Husbands are to love their wives as Christ loved the Church. The apostle, then, acts as a husband to the Church.

The scriptures give guidelines for how the husband is to treat his wife (Ephesians 5:22-32; I Peter 3:7). The same principles apply to the apostle.

**The Love of the Apostle**

Husbands must love their wives. Apostles

have a deep love for the Church. They minister in the Church with the love and compassion of Christ. Paul instructs husbands to love and lay down their lives for their wives as Christ did for the Church.

The apostle's life and ministry are set-aside for the Church and the advancement of the Kingdom of God. The scriptures tell us that Jesus became sin for us. He loved us so much that He became a curse in the eyes of man that we may live.

In the above verses, Paul gives an account to the Corinthian Church of how they are suffering many things for their sakes. Apostles are to lay down their lives for the Church, that the glory of God may be seen in her, Jesus said.

*Greater love hath no man than this, that a man lay down his life for his friends. (John*

*15:13)*

The greatest demonstration of love by Christ was that He gave His life for us. The apostle has to be willing to do the same for the Church.

**The Word and the Apostle**

Husbands must impart the Word to their wives. As Christ sanctified the Church by the Word, so should husbands be able to impart life to their wives by the Word. As husbands to the Church, apostles share in the responsibility of cleansing the Church through the Word, that she may be presented unto God without spot or winkle.

The focus of the apostle's ministry is to make ready a people for the coming of the Lord, and to present the Church to Christ as a chaste bride. This is accomplished through the preaching of the Word.

Consider the following:

> *Now ye are clean through the word which I have spoken unto you. (John 15:3)*
>
> *For I am jealous over you with godly jealousy: for I have espoused you to one husband, that I may present you as a chaste virgin to Christ. (II Corinthians 11:2)*

Jesus pronounced His disciples clean because He had preached the Word unto them. The apostle, like Christ, cleanses the Church through the Word.

**The Endearing Love**

Husbands must love their wives as their own bodies. Husbands are instructed to love their wives as their own bodies. Apostles have to minister with great love. Though they minister to the Church, they themselves are also a part of the

Church.

> *Husbands are admonished to nourish and cherish their wives as they would their own bodies.*

Apostles should remember to minister to the Church as if they are ministering to themselves. The apostles and the Church will stand before the judgment seat of God.

-Chapter 3-

# Building of the Apostle:

## Christ in Revelation

God develops humility and love in the apostle to build them into fruitful ambassadors. There are general characteristics that every apostle possesses as a result of Christ's building process.

Since the apostle will reflect Christ, Christ is God's prototype for building the apostle. John's vision of Christ in the book of Revelation gives a clear depiction of how God builds the apostle.

*And in the midst of the seven candlesticks one like unto the Son of man, clothed with a garment down to the foot, and girt about the paps with a golden girdle. His head and his hairs were white like wool, as white as snow; and his eyes were as a flame of fire; And his feet like unto fine brass, as if they burned in a furnace; and his voice as the sound of many waters. And he had in is mouth went a sharp two-edged sword: and his countenance was as the sun shineth in his strength. (Revelation 1:12-16)*

**Spiritual Consecration**

*Clothed with Linen Garment & Golden Belt.* The garments in the vision reflect the apostle's total consecration to God in ministry. In the Old Testament, the priests wore special garments to reflect their ministry.

The apostolic ministry is given to the Church as the priests were given to minister daily to the whole nation.

The linen reflects the purity that the apostle should have in ministry, while the gold belt is representative of the truth that he will carry.

*And thou shalt speak unto all that are wise hearted, whom I have filled with the spirit of wisdom, that they may make*

> Aaron's garments to consecrate him, that he may minister unto me in the priest's office. (Exodus 28:3)

## Spiritual Understanding

*Head and Hair White like Wool.* The white head and hair represent the wisdom and understanding that the apostle possesses. The apostles are stewards over the mysteries of God. The Lord will give them understanding of the deep things of God. Their doctrine will be sound, being able to mature the saints.

> Let a man so account of us, as of the ministers of Christ, and stewards of the mysteries of God. (I Corinthians 4:1)

## Spiritual Insight

*Eyes as a Flame of Fire.* The eyes of fire reflect the apostle's spiritual insight. It also represents the apostle's ability to see into the realm of the Spirit. The apostle will not only have revelation of the scriptures, but also have prophetic insight to enhance their ministries.

> *Which in other ages was not made known unto the sons of men, as it is now revealed unto his holy apostles and prophets by the Spirit. (Ephesians 3:5)*

**Spiritual Motivation**

*Feet like Fine Brass.* Feet like fine brass reflect the apostle's motivation in ministry. The feet carry us from one place to another. The Lord purifies the apostle's motivation in ministry that he will continually follow Christ. This is reflected in the brass feet being burned in the furnace.

> *I am crucified with Christ: nevertheless I live; yet not I, but Christ liveth in me: and the life which I now live in the flesh I live by the faith of the Son of God, who loved*

*me, and gave himself for me. (Galatians 2:20)*

In addition, the brass feet burned in a furnace reflects the zeal the apostle has for the Kingdom of God and the Church.

**Spiritual Speech**

*Voice like Many Waters.* The voice like many waters reflects the soundness of speech the apostle has.

The apostle will have understanding and the ability to communicate it.

*But we speak the wisdom of God in a mystery, even the hidden wisdom, which God ordained before the world unto our glory. (I Corinthians 2:7)*

In addition, the voice of many waters represents the scope of the apostle's ministry. His word will be to the Church as a whole. The apostle will be able to reach different kinds of peoples and nationalities (the many waters) with the message of the Kingdom of God.

**Spiritual Responsibility**

*Seven Stars in Hand.* The stars in the vision represented the seven churches. This reflects the apostle's responsibility to minister to the Church. His volition is the Church and the advancement of the Kingdom. It also reflects the apostle's influence on the Church.

> *The apostle has the Church's direction and growthin his hand through ministry.*
>
> *That ye may be mindful of the words which were spoken before by the holy prophets, and of the commandment of us the apostles of the Lord and Saviour. (2 Peter 3:2)*

**Spiritual Doctrine**

*Two-edged Sword in Mouth.* The sword in the mouth reflects the effectiveness of the apostle's preaching and teaching ministry. Their words will be able to cut to the heart and produce conviction in the listeners.

In addition, their words will inspire growth in the hearers. Their words will cut off "excess" that comes with religion to present Christ.

> *For the word of God is quick, and powerful, and sharper than any two-edged sword, piercing even to the dividing asunder of soul and spirit, and of the joints and marrow, and is a discerner of the thoughts and intents of the heart. (Hebrews 4:12)*

## Spiritual Reflection

*Countenance of Sun in Strength.* The countenance of the sun represents the apostle's responsibility to reflect Christ in his ministry. As the apostle executes his ministry, Jesus' image and brightness should always be seen and not the glory of the apostle.

*But God forbid that I should glory, save in the cross of our Lord Jesus Christ, by whom the world is crucified unto me, and I unto the world. (Galatians 6:14 Emphasis Mine)*

God humbles the apostle, produces love in the apostle, and builds him in Christ's image so that the apostle has the proper conduct and character in ministry.

-Chapter 4-

# The Apostle's Character:

## Fruit of the Spirit

The apostle's ministry is not only based upon what they do (which is subjective to the will of God), but also in who they are. Mature apostles are known primarily by their godly characters and secondarily by their ministries.

Before learning about the functions of the apostle in detail, the apostle's character has to be addressed.

> *But the fruit of the Spirit is love, joy, peace, longsuffering, gentleness, goodness, faith, meekness, temperance: against such there is no law. (Galatians 5:22-23)*

The apostle's character finds it definition within the person of Christ. To represent Christ fully, the apostle's character has to mirror the fruit of the Spirit. The fruit of the Spirit must then become the "fruit of apostolic character."

We have divided the fruit of the Spirit into three categories: The Attitude of the Spirit, The Empathy of the Spirit, and The Endurance of the Sprit.

**The Attitude of the Sprit**

Love, joy, and peace reflect the proper outlook and approach given by the Spirit for the apostle's success.

*Love*

Love has to be the foundation of the apostle's ministry. God is love. Christ demonstrated His love for us through His obedience to God and His death on the cross. God's involvement with men is always through His love. His correction and discipline is rooted in love. The apostle has to be the express image of God. No matter what his ministry entails, it must be done through love.

*Charity suffereth long, and is kind; charity envieth not; charity vaunteth not itself, is not puffed up, doth not behave itself unseemly, seeketh not her own, is not easily provoked, thinketh no evil; rejoiceth not in iniquity, but rejoiceth in the truth; Beareth all things, believeth all things, hopeth all things, endureth all things. (I Corinthians 13:4-7)*

The apostle has to have an everlasting love for God, the Church, and his family. If he rebukes, corrects, admonishes, teaches, warns, and prays, love has to be the source. The apostle's demonstration of love must match Paul's description of love as recorded in I Corinthians 13.

*Joy*

Apostles are carriers of the good news.

Though they are driven, they should also be men of joy. While writing to the Romans, Paul dealt with strife between believers over non-doctrinal issues. At the end of his discourse, he said these words,

> *For the kingdom of God is not eating and drinking, but righteousness, JOY, and peace in the Holy Spirit. (Romans 14:17 NASV Emphasis mine)*

The apostles possess the message of the kingdom. Part of that message is joy. They must teach believers how to remain joyful in the midst of adverse situations.

*Peace*

Apostles must be ministers of peace. Apostolic ministry puts them in the middle of conflict, but it must not be the result of the apostles' own personality traits. Apostles have to be led by peace and inspire peace in their audiences. Jesus prayed that we would have peace, though the gospel sets us against the world.

> *Peace I leave with you, my peace I give unto you: not as the world giveth, give I unto you. Let not your heart be troubled, neither let it be afraid. (John 14:27)*

Apostles, as senior representatives of Christ, must continue to remind the saints of the peace He left for them. In addition, apostles must not be angry, bitter, or harsh, but governed by peace.

**The Empathy of the Spirit**

The Spirit empowers the apostle to approach life under Jesus' command to wise as serpents and harmless as doves (Matthew 10:16).

*Patience*

Patience is one of the hallmarks of true

apostolic ministry. Apostles have to be men of patience as they minister to the Church. Patience is vital for this purpose-driven ministry. Apostles must have patience as they wait to see the fruits of their labors develop in the lives of believers. Paul spoke of this apostolic patience when he said,

> *I am become a fool in glorying; ye have compelled me: for I ought to have been commended of you: for in nothing am I behind the very chiefest apostles, though I be nothing. Truly the signs of an apostle were wrought among you in all patience, in signs, and wonders, and mighty deeds. For what is it wherein ye were inferior to other churches, except it be that I myself was not burdensome to you? Forgive me this wrong. (II Corinthians 12:11-13)*

Apostles are not to be "task masters" over the people of God. They must exercise patience as they execute their ministries.

*Kindness*

Apostles have to be kind. Because they exercise great authority in the Spirit, they have no excuse to be rude or mean. Some apostles use their ministries as an excuse for a lack of kindness.

> *For a bishop must be blameless, as the steward of God; not self-willed, not soon angry, not given to wine, no striker, not given to filthy lucre; (Titus 1:7)*
>
> *But a lover of hospitality, a lover of good men, sober, just, holy, temperate.(Titus1:8)*

Apostles have to know how to conduct themselves as recipients of the grace and mercy of God. With this understanding, their lives at home and among the saints must be in demonstration of the kindness of God.

## The Endurance of the Spirit

The Holy Spirit enables the apostle to remain faithful in service without becoming bitter and harsh.

*Faithfulness*

Every apostle must be faithful to the call of God. He must demonstrate loyalty to Christ and the Church. Apostles have to be unwavering in their commitment to God.

> *Let a man so account of us, as of the ministers of Christ, and stewards of the mysteries of God. (I Corinthians 4:1)Moreover, it is required in stewards, that a man be found faithful. (I Corinthians 4:2)*

Since apostolic ministry is confrontational, faithfulness will sustain the apostle in times of great adversity. One of God's attributes is faithfulness; therefore, the apostle has to be faithful as he carries out the will of God.

*Gentleness*

Apostles have to be gentle as they minister to the saints. They may have the right words, but the wrong delivery. In addition, they are to be gentle with family and friends. It is a required trait of the servant of the Lord.

> *And the servant of the Lord must not strive; but be gentle unto all men, apt to teach, patient, In meekness instructing those that oppose themselves; if God peradventure will give them repentance to the acknowledging of the truth. (II Timothy 2:24)*

*Self-Control*

Apostles are to exercise self-control in every affair of their lives. Self-control is needed in the pulpit, on the mission field, or in their homes.

> *Not given to wine, no striker, not greedy of filthy lucre; but patient, not a brawler, not covetous; one that ruleth well his own house, having his children in subjection with all gravity. (I Timothy 3:3-4)*

Anyone called to the apostolic ministry must remember that success in ministry is not in ministerial activities, but in the maintenance of character, integrity, and conduct. Godly character will determine the level of success of the apostles as they fulfill their functions in the Church.

**THE BELIEVER'S GUIDE TO THE APOSTOLIC MINISTRY** — A Comprehensive Study of the Apostolic Ministry in the Church

# -Book 2-
# The Apostle Question:

Exploring the Role of Apostles in the New Testament Church

The focus of this book is to bring clarity and understanding to the role of the apostle in the Church. Sound biblical answers to questions concerning the function of the apostle are answered. This information will help individuals to recognize the operations of this anointing in their lives and in the lives of others. It is our hope that believers will develop a greater respect and acceptance of the apostolic office and gift.

# Preface

Apostles and apostolic ministry are important to the furtherance of the Kingdom of God and the Church. It is my prayer that the information presented in this work will bring clarity, appreciation, and understanding to apostles and apostolic ministry.

Numerous works have been produced which highlight the ministry of the apostle. This book is to be used in connection with other publications. It is our prayer that those called to this office will gain insight for their ministries. In addition, I pray that others will develop an understanding of this ministry in the Church.

Roderick Levi Evans

# Introduction

At His departure, Jesus instructed the disciples to go to Jerusalem to await the promise of the Father. On the day of Pentecost, this promise was fulfilled with the outpouring of the Holy Spirit.

The Holy Spirit was given so that the work of Jesus Christ would continue on the earth. The Ministerial Endowments Series is designed to bring clarity to the gifts and ministries given to the Church. It is our prayer that believers will be enlightened and encouraged.

## In this publication:

Controversy over the gifts and ministries of the Spirit has abounded for centuries. Various scholars have taught that there was a cessation of the gifts and ministries. More specifically, they affirm that the ministry of the Apostle is no longer in operation nor valid. However, in recent years, a resurgence of the operation and demonstration of this ministry occurred. Traditional and Non-traditional churches, alike, have experienced the visitation of God through the Holy Spirit.

Since the emergence and acceptance of the ministries and gifts of the Holy Spirit, various authors have written concerning this phenomenon. In spite of this, many in the Church, presently, do not understand the functions and operations of, namely, the office of the Apostle. Even in organizations and denominations that consider this ministry valid today, comprehension is oftentimes elementary. Where there is no clear understanding, individuals become vulnerable to deception and error.

Since the apostolic office has authority and responsibility in the Kingdom of God, there are individuals in the Church who desire to function in this office. There are men and women who know they are not called to this office, yet they pursue it.

They lust after the respect that men have for those in this office. If they cannot be recognized as an apostle, some want to be identified with the office. Therefore, individuals resort to saying that they have an apostolic anointing upon their lives, without having any knowledge or understanding of the office or the anointing associated with it.

In this book, we will bring clarity to the role of the apostle in the New Testament Church. In addition, we will explain with simplicity the apostolic anointing. It is our prayer that believers will recognize the operation of this anointing in their lives and in the lives of others. We can be confident that God is still using His people in these last days.

-Chapter 1-

# What is an Apostle?

The first ministry to be on display in the New Testament Church was that of the apostle. The Book of Acts highlights the ministry of the apostles. Some biblical scholars have asserted that the only true apostles were the eleven disciples (excluding Judas Iscariot) with the exception of Paul.

Others have stated that the ministry of the apostles is useless since we have the canon of scripture. In addition, others promote that apostolic ministry ceased after the deaths of the first century apostles. As believers, we must understand that these teachings are erroneous.

***The ministry of the apostle is still vital and important to the advancement of the kingdom of God and the Church.*** Without this ministry, the Church cannot fulfill its mission in the earth.

*And He set some in the Church, first apostles... (I Corinthians 12:28)*

The word apostle originates from the Greek word *apostolos,* which means one who is sent forth. Apostles are sent from the presence of God with a divine message. They are sent forth for a specific task.

Not all apostles will discharge their duty in the same manner; neither will they all have the same anointing. Apostles' ministries will vary in demonstration and execution.

Though apostolic ministry seems exclusive to the New Testament, we discover from the scriptures that apostolic ministry was demonstrated in the Old Testament.

**Apostolic Ministry in the Old Testament**

The apostolic ministry is a foundational ministry (will be discussed later). The apostolic anointing is designed to bring people into the knowledge of God and Christ.

In the Old Testament, some men seemed to have an apostolic grace upon their lives. Two key biblical figures that exemplify this truth are Abraham and Moses.

Each of these men were prophets, but from God's interaction with them, we discover there was a type of apostolic anointing on their lives. They demonstrated three apostolic traits:

1) *They reflect the character of God.*
2) *They established individuals in the faith of God.*
3) *They exercised great spiritual authority and power.*

Abraham was sent to a foreign land by the command of God. Abraham received a commission as does an apostle.

*Now the Lord had said unto Abram, Get thee*

> *Get the out of thy country, and from thy kindred, and from thy father's house, unto a land that I will shew thee. (Genesis 12:1)*

The apostolic grace was evident in Abraham's life because it was through his life that foreigners were introduced to the God of heaven. The Lord magnified Himself in Abraham's life as he traveled throughout the land. We know that *Abraham's character reflected God's* as the apostle's does Christ. For God commanded him saying,

> *And when Abram was ninety years old and nine, the Lord appeared to Abram, and said unto him, I am the Almighty God; walk before me, and be thou perfect. (Genesis 17:1)*

Like the modern-day apostle, *Abraham was used to establish the faith of God* in his descendants and in the earth. As apostles are fathers in the Spirit, Abraham is the father of faith.

> *And God said unto Abraham, Thou shalt keep my covenant therefore, thou and thy seed after thee in their generations. (Genesis 17:9)*

Finally, Abraham exercised great authority and power. After God rebuked Abimelech for Sarah's sake, He told the king that Abraham would pray for him and the barrenness of his household would end. As apostles exercise great power, so did Abraham through his praye

> *So Abraham prayed unto God: and God healed Abimelech, and his wife, and his maidservants; and they bare children. For the Lord had fast closed up all the wombs of the house of Abimelech, because*

*of Sarah Abraham's wife. (Genesis 20;17-18)*

Moses, like Abraham demonstrated apostolic grace. When God spoke of his ministry, He said that Moses was not like other prophets. **Apostles and prophets are similar, but the apostle's ministry is greater than the prophet's because of the spiritual authority of the office.** This is what Moses represented in his day. He was a prophet, but there was something greater about him.

*And he said, Hear now my words: If there be a prophet among you, I the Lord will make myself known unto him in a vision, and will speak unto him in a dream. My servant Moses is not so, who is faithful in all mine house. (Numbers 12:6-7)*

When God sent Moses to Pharaoh, He told

Moses that Aaron would be his prophet, and Moses would be as God to Pharaoh. This is a clear demonstration of the apostolic grace. Moses would reflect God's character as he fulfilled his ministry. Numerous biblical accounts recall the power that Moses exercised. Signs and wonders surrounded his ministry to the Jews. This is parallel to the ministry of the apostles.

Finally, like the modern-day apostle, Moses established people in the faith of God. The apostles laid a spiritual foundation for the Church to grow upon while Moses instituted the Law from God to set up the Levitical priesthood and Israelite worship.

From these two patriarchs, we see a demonstration and foreshadowing of the apostolic ministry to come under the New Covenant.

## Apostolic Ministry in the New Testament

After the establishment of the Church, God used apostles. ***The apostle is sent as a chief representative of Christ.*** They represent the person of Christ to the Church and world (however, this is done alongside other believers and ministers). They are preachers of the Gospel of Jesus Christ.

Apostles mature believers in their walks with the Lord. They serve as spiritual fathers. They have the grace upon their lives to establish order to the worship of God. In addition, they have prophetic insight and great authority in the realm of the Spirit.

In addition to the above functions, the New Testament apostle serves as a foundational ministry to the Church. On the day of Pentecost, God established His will for man's worship. He no longer wanted to be "confined" to a building (represented by God's command to worship at the Temple), but dwell in the hearts of man. His will was for the believer to be His temple.

As He abides in each individual, they corporately become the temple of God. Peter called the believers "stones" who are built together to form a spiritual house or temple where God could dwell.

*Ye also, as lively stones, are built up a spiritual house, an holy priesthood, to offer up spiritual sacrifices, acceptable to God by Jesus Christ. (I Peter 2:5)*

*What? Know ye not that your body is the temple of the Holy Ghost which is in you, which ye have of God, and ye are not your own? (I Corinthians 6: 19)*

With the New Covenant, the temple of God is now the hearts and minds of people. Their actual bodies become the habitation of God. Therefore, if the Church consists of people joined together by the presence of the Holy Spirit, then the foundation for the Church would consist of people.

As Paul wrote to the believers, he revealed to them a very important truth. He told them that they (the Church) were built upon the foundation of the **apostles** and prophets with Christ being the head stone.

> *Now therefore ye are no more strangers and foreigners, but fellowcitizens with the saints, and of the household of God; And are built upon the foundation of the apostles and prophets, Jesus Christ himself being the chief corner stone; In whom all*

*the building fitly framed together groweth unto an holy temple in the Lord: In whom ye also are builded together for an habitation of God through the Spirit. (Ephesians 2:19-22).*

In the above scripture, we discover certain truths. Paul was writing to a primarily Gentile audience. However, we must understand that the foundation that they stood upon was the same as the Jewish believers. Jewish and Gentile believers, alike, operated in the foundation established by the New Testament **apostles** and prophets.

The Church, like the New Covenant, was founded upon people, namely, the **apostles** and prophets. From this, we understand that since we will reign with Christ, God allowed man to have an active role in the establishment of the

Church. The **apostles** and prophets bear the responsibility for the Church, especially in doctrinal purity and spiritual direction. As Christ formed the foundation for the New Covenant, the **apostles** and prophets formed the foundation for the Church. *Their ministries are foundational and continue to be major influences upon the Body of Christ.*

The ministries of the **apostles** and prophets were needed to establish the Church, and their ministries are needed presently for the furtherance of the Church. Christ's ministry toward us is everlasting.

> *But this man, because he continueth ever, hath an unchangeable priesthood. Wherefore he is able also to save them to the uttermost that come unto God by him, seeing he ever liveth to make*

*intercession for them. (Hebrews 7:24-25)*

The Book of Acts reveals to us that the ministries of the apostles were essential in the establishment of the Church and the advancement of the Kingdom of God. Consider the following Signs and wonders accompanied the apostles' ministries to confirm the message that they preached. This helps to advance the Kingdom of God.

*And fear came upon every soul: and many wonders and signs were done by the apostles. (Acts 2:43)*

*God also bearing them witness, both with signs and wonders, and with divers miracles, and gifts of the Holy Ghost, according to his own will. (Hebrews 2:4)*

The apostles' ministries were vital to establishing the Church and believers in the faith.

> And they continued stedfastly in the apostles' doctrine and fellowship, and in breaking of bread, and in prayers. (Acts 2:42)
>
> This second epistle, beloved, I now write unto you; in both which I stir up your pure minds by way of remembrance: That ye may be mindful of the words which were spoken before by the holy prophets, and of the commandment of us the apostles of the Lord and Saviour. (2 Peter 3:1-2)

Not only did the New Testament apostles reveal future events and encourage the brethren, but also, they helped to set up elders and pastors in the Church.

> For this cause left I thee in Crete, that thou shouldest set in order the things that

*are wanting, and ordain elders in every city, as I had appointed thee. (Titus 1:5)*

From the above scriptures and references, we discover that the New Testament Church has apostles, individuals who possess as apostolic anointing, and those who have and apostolic gift. These gifts were needed then and they are needed now.

There are some theologians who twist the scriptures. They assert that because we have the canon of scripture, apostles and apostolic ministry are no longer needed. The scriptures declare that Jesus Christ is the same yesterday, today, and forever (Hebrews 13:8).

He ministered to the early Church through the apostles. He will not change until the end of all things. If He used apostles and apostolic ministry in those times, He will continue to do so.

Christ's ministry to the Church will not end until the Judgment; therefore, the ministries of the apostles will not end until that Day. God is still using apostles today. In addition, God is raising up individuals who walk under and in an apostolic anointing that His glory may be seen in all.

-Chapter 2-
# The Call of an Apostle

God calls individuals to the apostolic office in many ways. In the Old and New Testaments, we discover that God called men in different manners. God's call to the apostolic office is an undeniable call. The apostle's ministry is needed if the Church is going to mature and the Kingdom of God is to advance. Therefore, God establishes them in their work through His calling. There are individuals calling themselves apostles without having a definite call from the Lord or confirmation from among the brethren.

This chapter is designed to help believers recognize the apostolic calling upon others and themselves. We will look at scriptural examples of how the Lord called individuals to understand the call of the apostle.

**Acknowledging the Apostolic Call**

The call of an apostle is unique from others

in one respect. Though all ministers receive their calling from the Lord, the apostolic call comes with a revelation of Christ. Since the New Testament highlights the ministry of the apostles, we will use examples from these texts to understand the apostle's call.

*Jesus & the Twelve*

After His ministry began, Jesus called men to walk aside Him. These men were later called apostles.

> *And when it was day, he called unto him his disciples: and of them he chose twelve, whom also he named apostles. (Luke 6:13)*

This verse gives us an extremely important truth concerning apostles. **ONLY JESUS CAN CALL APOSTLES.** Serving an apostle does not make one a candidate for this ministry. A prophetic word does not make one an apostle, except it is truly from the Lord.

Desiring this office greatly does not signify a call to this office. Jesus will call and ordain apostles personally. After His calling, there will be confirmation of it in the Church. In the book of John, we discover that after John the Baptist revealed whom Christ was, two of his disciples left to follow Jesus.

*Again the next day after John stood, and two of his disciples; And looking upon Jesus as he walked, he saith, Behold the Lamb of God! And the two disciples heard him speak, and they followed Jesus. (John 1:35-37)*

**The apostolic call does not begin with the apostle fulfilling a ministry, but it begins with a revelation of Jesus.** When John and

Andrew discovered who Christ was, they immediately followed Him. Jesus did not call them, but they pursued. Individuals who are called to the apostleship usually are concerned with following and pleasing Christ above a calling to a ministry. This is a part of their calling. If they cannot follow the person of Christ, they will not be able to represent Him, as they should in ministry.

The apostle's call normally begins with an inward conviction and witness before an external experience is given. Continuing our examination of the twelve, we discover that Jesus called them personally also.

> *And going on from thence, he saw other two brethren, James the son of Zebedee, and John his brother, in a ship with Zebedee their father, mending their nets; and he*

*called them. And they immediately left the ship and their father and followed him. (Matthew 4:18-22)*

*And as he passed by, he saw Levi the son of Alphaeus sitting at the receipt of custom, and said unto him, Follow me. And he arose and followed him. (Mark 2:14)*

**The apostle's call will be a personal one. He will be brought face to face with Jesus Christ.** The apostle's call begins with a revelation of Jesus and then a time of following Him in service. The apostles followed Him and ministered unto Him before they operated in full apostolic authority.

Any individual claiming to have an apostolic call without a servant's heart is probably not called of God. The apostles willingly served Jesus.

When we consider the conversion of Saul, we discover that Jesus called Him in a similar manner. Before He received His calling, he received a personal encounter and revelation of Jesus.

> *And he fell to the earth, and heard a voice saying unto him, Saul, Saul, why persecutest thou me? And he said, Who art thou, Lord? And the Lord said, I am Jesus whom thou persecutest: it is hard for thee to kick against the pricks. And he trembling and astonished said, Lord, what wilt thou have me to do? And the Lord said unto him, Arise, and go into the city, and it shall be told thee what thou must do. (Acts 9:4-6)*

Because of the future apostolic ministry, we find that Saul's response to the Lord was like the other apostles. After Jesus told Him who He was, his next response was an inquiry, as to what the Lord wanted Him to do.

Saul did not wrestle or fight, he immediately expressed his desire to obey and follow Christ. After demonstrating his willingness to follow Him, Saul received an understanding and confirmation of his call to ministry.

> *And one Ananias, a devout man according to the law, having a good report of all the Jews which dwelt there, Came unto me, and stood, and said unto me, Brother Saul, receive thy sight. And the same hour I looked up upon him. And he said, The God of our fathers hath chosen thee, that thou shouldest know his will, and see that Just One, and shouldest hear the voice of his mouth. For thou shalt be his witness unto all men of*

*what thou hast seen and heard. (Acts 22:12-15)*

The modern-day apostle's calling will come in a similar manner. He will be consumed with following Christ. As a result, he will experience an encounter with the Lord that will substantiate his ministry. After these things, there will be confirmation through the brethren.

**Answering the Apostolic Call**

Once an individual receives a call to the apostolic office, there must be a response and answer to the Lord. Before the apostle's making (discussed in the next chapter) begins, there are certain things that the future apostle has to do.

*Seek Servanthood*

The apostle's office comes with great authority and power. The apostle has to guard his spirit against arrogance and pride. A sure way of this is to develop a servant's heart He should seek opportunities to serve. Since apostles are called at different times in their lives and ministries, this can be difficult.

> But he that is greatest among you shall be your servant. (Matthew 23:11)

Some individuals receive a call to the apostolic office after being in ministry for years. In this instance, the individual needs to find someone they can submit to and serve in order to prepare for the budding apostolic ministry. Jesus demonstrated the level of humility that an apostle needs when He washed the disciples' feet.

> So after he had washed their feet, and had taken his garments, and was set down again, he said unto them, Know ye what I have done to you? Ye call me Master and Lord: and ye say well; for so I am. If I then,

*your Lord and Master, have washed your feet; ye also ought to wash one another's feet. For I have you an example, that ye should do as I have done to you. (John 13:12-15)*

Jesus showed the apostles that even though they would have great power and authority, they should be willing to serve even in the lowest forms. The apostles received this lesson well.

Even after Pentecost and expansion of the Church through their miraculous ministry, the apostles still served food to the widows (Acts 6:1-8). Though they healed the sick, raised the dead, and preached the Gospel, they were still servants. It was only after the service hindered their ministry that they appointed others to serve the widows for them.

*Seek Solitude*

After receiving notice of a call to the apostolic, a time of separation is needed to ensure the apostle's success. The separation does not necessarily have to be physical, but definitely spiritual. The apostle has to take time to seek the Lord and receive revelation from Jesus concerning His Church. After his conversion and calling, Paul experienced a time of separation in order to be instructed of the Lord.

> *But when it pleased God, who separated me from my mother's womb, and called me by his grace, To reveal his Son in me, that I might preach him among the heathen; immediately I conferred not with flesh and blood: Neither went I up to Jerusalem to them which were apostles before me; but I went into Arabia, and returned again unto*

*Damascus. Then after three years I went up to Jerusalem to see Peter, and abode with him fifteen days. (Galatians 1:15-18)*

Paul wrote that when God wanted to reveal Christ to him, he went into Arabia and then Damascus over the space of three years. He wrote that he did not discuss it men, he allowed the Lord to minister unto him. After the Lord was finished, Paul spoke to other apostles to verify the things he had received.

The modern-day apostle will be called into a time of solitude with the Lord. During this time, the Lord will correct erroneous beliefs and doctrines so that the apostle can fully reflect Christ in his doctrine and ministry. *The information that the apostle receives during this time will not divide the Church or be "brand new."*

When Paul conferred with the other apostles, they verified that the things he preached were of the Lord. God will confirm the apostle's revelation (usually through other apostles).

*Seek Sanctification*

A call to the apostolic office is an invitation to spiritual warfare. If the enemy cannot stop the individual's resolve to serve the Lord, he will weaken the future apostle's ministry through ungodliness. Therefore, the apostle has to seek sanctification; that is, a life of holiness to ensure success in the ministry.

> *But I keep under my body, and bring it into subjection: lest that by any means, when I have preached to others, I myself should be a castaway. (I Corinthians 9:27)*

Paul, after years of ministry, confessed that he still had to bring his body (flesh and its lusts) under subjection. The apostle's quest for holiness **increases** at the reception of his calling and **continues** during its fulfillment.

**Accepting the Apostolic Call**

Since the apostolic office invites controversy, there is confusion as to how to recognize and accept the apostolic calling in our lives and in the lives of others. Therefore, in concluding our examination of the call of an apostle, we will discuss briefly certain signs of the apostolic calling. This will help in the acceptance of the apostolic call on an individual's life.

*Revelation of Jesus Christ*

The individual who is called to the apostolic office will have a profound understanding of Jesus Christ. He will speak of Christ in the most personal terms. Christ will reveal Himself to the apostolic individual through dreams and visions, through the voice of the Spirit, or through the scriptures.

Regardless of the method used, the apostolic individual will have a clear revelation of Christ and

His work.

> *Am I not an apostle? am I not free? Have I not seen Jesus Christ our Lord? Are not ye my work in the Lord? (I Corinthians 9:1)*

We must remember that all believers are to know Christ. God will reveal a deep understanding of Christ to whom He will. Though the apostle will have this level of understanding, any believer is a candidate for it. Again, this is given as a sign of a call to the apostolic office.

*Consistent Intercession*

Apostles have a deep love for Christ and

the Church. Because of this, those who are called to this office will have consistent prayer lives. Much of their prayer will be for the Church, its members, and its advancement. They have a desire to see Christ's rule in the earth. In his letters, the apostle Paul would tell the churches of his constant intercession for them. This is a sure sign of the apostolic calling.

> *For this cause we also, since the day we heard it, do not cease to pray for you, and to desire that ye might be filled with the knowledge of his will in all wisdom and spiritual understanding. (Colossians 1:9)*

Conversely, we know that Jesus challenges all believers to be consistent in prayer. In addition, the scriptures continually admonish believers to be intercessors for one another. Again, consistent intercession may be a sign of the apostolic office, not the manifestation of it.

*Authority in the Spirit*

One of the sure signs of an apostolic call is the presence of great authority in the Spirit. Those who called to the apostolic office will have the revelation gifts of the Spirit operating in them consistently. In addition, they will possess the power gifts of healing and working of miracles. They will be effective in the casting out of demons.

> *Truly the signs of an apostle were wrought among you in all patience, in signs, and wonders, and mighty deeds. (2 Corinthians 12:12)*

The revelation and power of the Spirit is available to all Christians. Jesus said that miraculous signs would follow anyone who believed on Him. Therefore, it is not uncommon to see believers who are not called to the apostolic possessing great power and authority. The presence of power and authority, again, is only a sign of the apostolic call.

We have already established that **ONLY JESUS CAN CALL APOSTLES.** The above signs are only indications of an apostolic call. Once an apostolic call is established, the apostle goes through training and discipline. In the next chapter, we will discuss the making of an apostle.

Exercising great power and authority in the Spirit is not the hallmark of the apostle's ministry; it is his character. Therefore, Christ builds the apostle to reflect His nature.

**THE BELIEVER'S GUIDE TO THE APOSTOLIC MINISTRY** — A Comprehensive Study of the Apostolic Ministry in the Church

-Chapter 3-
# The Office of the Apostle

Though there are varieties of ministries and operations, apostles have essentially the same functions.

**Nine Functions of the Apostle**

Some functions are not exclusive to apostles. However, apostles will differ from other ministries in the execution of those functions.

**Preach & Teach the Word of God (I Tim. 2:7).** Apostles are gifted to preach and/or teach the word of God under divine inspiration and authority. They are anointed to make known the mysteries of God through the Word. This is performed with boldness and sobriety.

> *Let a man so account of us (apostles), as of the ministers of Christ, and stewards of the mysteries of God. (I Corinthians4:1 Parenthesis mine)*

**Impart Spiritual Gifts (Acts 8:17; Romans 1:11; II Tim. 1:6).** Apostles have the ability to bring forth the gifts of God in believers. They have the power to impart wisdom, knowledge, and understanding.

Apostles can bring to light the spiritual gifts resident in believers and impart gifts (by revelation of the Spirit) through the laying on of hands.

*Neglect not the gift that is in thee, which was given thee by prophecy, with the laying on of the hands of the presbytery. (I Timothy 4:14)*

**Establish and/or Oversee Churches and Organizations.** Because apostles are sent with a divine message, God uses some to start organizations as vehicles to present their messages.

In addition, apostles will start new churches and ministries in areas where they are sent to preach. This is to give structure to those who have heard the message. For example, Paul and Barnabas started many churches to give the new converts some organization to the worship of God.

> *And some days after Paul said unto Barnabas, Let us go again and visit our brethren in every city where we have preached the word of the Lord, and see how they do. (Acts 15:36)*

**Evangelize.** Every apostle has a message. Apostles are gifted to go into areas that have not been open to the gospel or areas that are stagnant. Jesus sent the original twelve out to preach. Every apostle will function as an evangelist, whether to the Church (to bring balance and order) or to the lost (for redemption and salvation).

> *For so hath the Lord commanded us, saying, I have set thee to be a light of the Gentiles, that thou shouldest be for salvation unto the ends of the earth. And when the Gentiles heard this, they were glad, and glorified the word of the Lord: and as many as were ordained to eternal life believed. And the word of the Lord was published throughout all the region. (Acts 13:47-49)*

**Raise Up Leaders (Acts 15:39; II Tim. 2:1-2; Acts 6:3-6).** Because of the authority given to them, apostles have the anointing and responsibility to raise up leaders. This is done for the advancement of the kingdom of God.

Apostles will have "Timothys" and "Elishas" in ministry so that the work of the Lord will continue after they have left the scene. If an apostle is the head of a religious organization, he will have the ability to recognize gifts and ministries in individuals and set them in the Church as directed by the Spirit.

*To Titus, mine own son after the common faith: Grace, mercy, and peace, from God the Father and the Lord Jesus Christ our Saviour. For this cause left I thee in Crete, that thou shouldest set in order the things that are wanting, and ordain elders in every city, as I had appointed thee. (Titus 1:4-5)*

**Expose False Apostles & Doctrine.** Apostles are stewards of over the mysteries of God. They have the wisdom and foresight to warn against deception. They will contend for purity of faith and doctrine in the Church. They, like the prophets of old, will warn and speak against false apostles openly.

> But there were false prophets also among the people, even as there shall be false teachers among you, who privily shall bring in damnable heresies, even denying the Lord that bought them, and bring upon themselves swift destruction. And many shall follow their pernicious ways; by reason of whom the way of truth shall be evil spoken of. (II Peter 2:1-2)

**Perform Signs, Wonders, Healings, & Miracles.** The apostle has a miraculous ministry. Apostles are gifted men, not only to perform signs and wonders, but in the revelation gifts of the Spirit. The word of knowledge, word of wisdom, discerning of spirits, and prophecy will operate regularly in their ministries.

> *And fear came upon every soul; and many wonders and signs were done by the apostles. (Acts 2:43)*

**Lay Spiritual Foundations in the Church.** Apostles have the authority and anointing to lay spiritual foundations in the Church. Though no modern-day apostles will write scripture, they are equipped to reveal the hidden truths of God's Word and lay the proper foundation for the people of God to grow thereby.

> *Whereby, when ye read, ye may understand my knowledge in the mystery of Christ) which in other ages was not made known unto the sons of men, as it is now revealed unto his holy apostles and prophets by the Spirit. (Ephesians 3:4-5)*

**Establish Churches in the Faith (Gospel).** Apostles have the unique ability to bring people back to the purity of the faith. They are able to instruct babes in Christ until they become mature in their personal relationships with God and in their doctrinal beliefs. They can promote stability and growth in the Body of Christ.

> *And as they went through the cities, they delivered them the decrees for to keep, that were ordained of the apostles and elders which were at Jerusalem. And so were the churches established in the faith and increased in number daily. (Acts 16:4-5)*

Though there are many dimensions to this awesome ministry (not listed), most apostles will demonstrate all of these functions at some time in their ministries.

**Focus of Apostles**

The focus and thrust of apostles is reflective of the role of the heart in the human body. The heart is the central location for where blood is pumped to the rest of the body. It is said to house our innermost feelings and emotions.

Apostles endeavor to reveal to the Church the heart of God. They have a love for God and strive to make others aware of the love of God towards them. Apostles strive to see the Church advance in the Kingdom of God. In the same manner that the heart pumps blood throughout the Body, they will make sure believers walk in the newness of life by their continual ministering in the Church. Though apostles have a zeal for order and structure in the Church, it must be balanced by love.

Apostolic individuals will know how to express the innermost heart of God and bring people into a father-child relationship with the

Lord. At the core, apostles want to see men and women be conformed to the likeness and image of Christ. The heart of God from the beginning was to have sons and daughters. The apostolic ministry is given to see this fulfilled in this life.

-Chapter 4-
# The Roles of the Apostle

We have examined what an apostle is and the call and functions of an apostle. At this time, we will explore the apostle's role in the Church. There is a diversity in the demonstration and expression of apostolic ministry. Apostolic ministry manifests itself in various ways.

However, there is some common ground among all apostles. No matter what their specific call is, apostles will exhibit characteristics of ambassadors, fathers, and husbands as they minister in the Church.

**Apostles as Ambassadors**

Every apostle is unique in his ministry. However, the apostle's role in the kingdom of God may parallel an ambassador's role in any earthly kingdom. Ambassadors are important to any nation. Oftentimes, they carry the nation's peace, prosperity, and safety by their words and actions.

Though every member of the Body of Christ functions as an ambassador for Him at some time, it is the primary role of the apostle. Paul compared apostolic ministry to that of an ambassador.

> *So, we as Christ's ambassadors, God making His appeal as it were through us. We {as Christ's personal representative} beg you for His sake to lay hold of the divine power [now offered you] and be reconciled to God. (II Corinthians 5:20 Amplified)*

**Ambassadors are the highest officials and/or representatives in government.** The word translated ambassador in the New Testament comes from the Greek word "presbeuo." It means to be a senior representative. Therefore, we conclude that among those God call into ministry, the apostle is the senior representative of the kingdom of God.

od set the apostles in the Church first, so that they could function as the ambassadors of the kingdom of God to the world's kingdom. They above all the other ministers must represent the kingdom of God as if Christ were still in the earth.

**Ambassadors are sent forth with specific guidelines of the one who sent them.** An ambassador does not choose what his assignment is. The ruler or government decides this. An ambassador does not become or function as an ambassador unless designated. The same is true for the apostle. The Lord appoints an apostle.

Individuals cannot lay claim to this office because of gifts, talents, and the advice of men. Jesus chose the apostles. If someone feels called to this office, the Lord will make it clear. However, one must remember that every apostle has a specific call on his life. Though he has great authority, only God directs him as to how to administer it.

**Ambassador's influence is limited to that given by ruler or government.** An ambassador only has influence in the countries that his government gives him. For instance, an ambassador to China may not have the same influence in Japan, if not sanctioned by the sending government.

Apostles only have authority over what God gives them. An apostle over one organization cannot assume apostleship over any organization or people in the Kingdom of God. God, alone, gives him his sphere of influence.

Some apostolic ministers have ignored this

fact and tried to usurp authority in churches and organizations where the Lord has not sent them. The apostle only has authority and influence in the places where God has sent them.

**Ambassador's words are equal to the one that sent them.** When ambassadors are commissioned, they are to speak as the ruler or government. Wars have begun and ended because of decisions made by the ambassadors. Above all the other offices, the apostles are to represent the voice of Christ and be in his stead as they minister in the Church.

Apostles are expected to speak and act even as Christ would. Apostles have to possess the nature of Christ. The apostle's actions have to be a reflection of the mind of Christ operating in them. (I Corinthians 2:16)

**Ambassadors have an invested/inherent authority.** Ambassadors are sent out with all authority and power of the commissioning government. Since they stand in place of the governing leadership, they walk in their power. Ambassadors are given this authority that they may fulfill their commission. Ambassadors cannot assume authority that is not given to them.

Apostles also have an invested authority. Their authority does not come because of what they do or who they are. Apostles do not have authority because they are apostles, but because God gives it to them. Apostles have to resist the temptation to abuse the authority God gives them.

> *For though I should boast somewhat more of our authority, which the Lord hath given us for edification, and not for your*

*destruction, I should not be ashamed. (II Corinthians 10:8)*

If apostles abuse their authority, it will result in the destruction of the Body of Christ. There are numerous accounts in the Church today of apostles who misuse their power.

**Ambassadors are expected to have wisdom, counsel, and knowledge of their ruler.** Ambassadors are entrusted with the responsibility of representing those who sent them. Therefore, the training and discipline placed upon them is great. They must have personal integrity and character. In addition, they must be able to represent those who have commissioned them with knowledge and dignity.

Apostles are no different. They, too, must possess the wisdom, knowledge, and personality of Christ. Because they walk in the very authority of Christ, the training and discipline of God is oftentimes grave.

This discipline is mandated, so that when they speak, they will speak as an oracle of God, even more so, they will speak in Christ's stead.

**Apostles as Fathers**

The role of an apostle in the Church is not only to be an ambassador for Christ, but also to serve as a "father" ministry. The apostle's role in the kingdom is similar to that of a father. The apostles, themselves, referred to themselves as fathers and to those who partook of their ministry as their children.

While writing to the Corinthian church, Paul likened his ministry unto a father. John called the saints his children.

*For if you were to have countless tutors in Christ, yet you would not have many*

> *fathers; for in Christ Jesus I became your father through the gospel. (I Corinthians 4:15 NASV)*
>
> *My little children, these things write I unto you, that ye sin not. And if any man sin, we have an advocate with the Father, Jesus Christ the righteous. (I John 2:1)*

The apostle will love the Church as a father loves his children. His personality in the Church will resemble that of a father.

**Fathers provide for their children.** As an earthly father provides for the needs of his children, the apostle will supply the spiritual needs of those entrusted to him. He will endeavor to ensure that the Church has the right information to live in this world in victory. They will strive to lay proper foundations in the lives of the people of God; that they may inherit the kingdom of God. Paul wrote,

> *Behold, the third time I am ready to come to you; and I will not be burdensome to you: for I seek not yours, but you: for the children ought not to lay up for the parents, but the parent for the children. And I will very gladly spend and be spent for you though the more abundantly I love you, the less I be loved. (II Corinthians 12:14-15)*

He explained to those at Corinth that as a father works and provides (spends) for his children, so he labors and expends his time, energy, and effort to provide for them spiritually. He wanted their souls to be saved. Apostles have to avoid becoming "lord" and "kings" over the people of God. God has set them in the Church to serve.

**Fathers nurture their children.** Though a father provides for his children, provision without nurture handicaps a child. An apostle must not only labor in the Church, his labor has to be goal oriented. Whatever the apostle's specific call is, his concern will be a personal one.

> But I (Paul and other apostles) proved to be gentle among you, as a nursing mother tenderly cares for her own children. (I Thessalonians 2:7 NASV, Parenthesis mine)

The apostle's personal concern has to be tempered with grace and patience. Because God uses them to bring order and stability, some apostles become harsh in their words and demeanor. The anointing of God is not to be blamed for character flaws.

**Fathers discipline their children.** If a child has

no discipline or training, he is liable to develop into a corrupt adult. The same is true for believers. If Christians are not disciplined, they will not grow up into mature saints. Apostles will execute judgment and discipline in the Church. However, love demonstrated this apostolic authority in his third epistle.

> *For this reason, if I come, I will call attention to his deeds which he does, unjustly accusing us with the wicked words; and not satisfied with this, neither does he himself receive the brethren, and he forbid those who desire to do so, and puts them out of the Church. (3 John verse 10 NASV)*

John says that he will "call attention" to what a divisive minister did. He was expressing that he would personally deal with the individual because of his error. Paul, on numerous occasions, exercised judgment and meted out discipline in the Church. While away from Corinth, news reached him that a brother was sleeping with this stepmother. He not only rebuked the church for not handling the situation, but also gave instruction concerning the discipline of the brother.

> *It is reported commonly that there is fornication among you, and such fornication as is not so much as named among the Gentiles, that one should have his father's wife. And ye are puffed up, and have not rather mourned, that he that hath done this deed might be taken away from among you. For I verily, as absent in body, but present in spirit, have judged already, as though I were present, concerning him that hath so done this deed, In the name*

*of our Lord Jesus Christ, when ye are gathered together, and my spirit, with the power of our Lord Jesus Christ, To deliver such an one unto Satan for the destruction of the flesh, that the spirit may be saved in the day of the Lord Jesus. (I Corinthians 5:1-5)*

Paul meted out discipline. However, it was for the salvation of the offender. True fathers discipline their children to save them. When the apostle rebukes, it has to be done in love, else he will offend one of God's very own. He must remember that he has a Father in heaven.

**Fathers give wise/sound instruction to their children.** The book of Proverbs is a compilation of instructions that a father would give to his children. Fathers seek to instill knowledge in their children. A father will pass on the information that he has learned. Apostles will impart revelation and knowledge to the Church as a father does to his children.

*And they continued stedfastly in the apostles' doctrine and fellowship, and in breaking of bread, and in prayers. (Acts 2:42)*

*But, beloved, remember ye the words which were spoken before of the apostles of our Lord Jesus Christ. (Jude verse 17)*

The Church was established on the apostle's teaching. Peter instructed them to remember what had been previously taught. He did not cite the teaching of other elders and leaders, but what the apostles taught. Apostles are expected to give fatherly wisdom and instruction in the Church.

-Chapter 5-
# Apostles in Perspective

The increase of revelation and information opens up the path to deception through excess As we endeavor to learn more about God and His ministries, we must avoid extremes. History has shown that every time God has moved in the earth, the enemy has tried to counterattack with excess and deception. We see this trend today with the emerging apostolic ministries.

In this chapter, we will endeavor to bring balance to the numerous teachings surrounding apostles. In short, we want to keep our outlook on the office in perspective.

**Apostles and the Church**

In the first chapter, we stated that apostolic ministry is a foundational ministry in the Church. Foundational does not mean that this ministry is more important or valuable than other ministries. When considering a building, the foundation is not seen. However, when storms and other influences come against the building, the foundation's strength provides support for the building.

The same is true for the Church. When apostles minister properly, they will not be the center of attention, but the entire Church will display the nature of Christ and the power of God. The true purpose of apostles is that their ministries help the Church stand against attacks of the enemy and deception. However, we see that the Church has lost vision, purpose, and power. This is because true apostolic ministry is missing.

Consequently, the Church promotes false doctrines and ministers unwittingly. In addition, it is divided over unimportant issues. The Church has left the simplicity of Christ to follow another gospel, based upon prosperity and not righteousness.

> *But I fear, lest by any means, as the serpent beguiled Eve through his subtilty, so your minds should be corrupted from the simplicity that is in Christ. For if he that cometh preacheth Jesus, whom we have not preached, or if ye receive another spirit, which ye have not received, or another gospel, which ye have not accepted, ye might well bear with him. (II Corinthians 11:3-4)*

The error of many apostles is that they have drawn attention to themselves and their gifts and have neglected their responsibilities to the Church. As a result, the whole Church suffers. Apostles are to minister so that the Church may shine.

> *For all things are for your sakes, that the abundant grace might through the thanksgiving of many redound to the glory of God. (II Corinthians 4:15)*
>
> *Therefore, I endure all things for the elect's sakes, that they may also obtain the salvation which is in Christ Jesus with eternal glory. (II Timothy 2:10)*

Modern-day apostles are to have this mentality as they minister. They minister so the Church would remain partakers of the grace of God unto salvation. The foundation supports the building. When apostles fulfill their tasks, local assemblies, churches, and organizations are healthy and vibrant.

The problem remains that individuals in the Body of Christ are exalting apostles, prophets, and other ministers above measure in the Church.

The Church has to be sober in its acceptance of apostles. They have to remember that apostles are individuals redeemed by Christ. Their gifts do not make them special or superior.

Their gifts and ministries make them responsible for the Church. Many apostles fall into pride and rebellion because men esteem them too highly. What, then, is to be the Church's approach to apostles?

> *For I say, through the grace given unto me, to every man that is among you, not to think of himself more highly than he ought to think; but to think soberly, according as God hath dealt to every man the measure of faith. For as we have many members in one body, and all members have not the same office: So we, being many, are one body in Christ,*

> *and every one members one of another. (Romans 12:3-5)*

Paul instructed the Romans that they were not to think too much of themselves. However, we must remember not to think too much of apostles. Why? He goes on to say that God has given every man a measure of faith to operate in whatever ministry or gift he has.

Therefore, since God is the source of all gifts, there is no need for the saints to think of anyone too highly. Yet, we are to give respect and honor unto one another as members of Christ.

> *Render therefore to all their dues: tribute to whom tribute is due; custom to whom custom; fear to whom fear; honour to whom honour. (Romans 13:7)*

Paul told the Romans that they were to give respect unto the leaders in government. Whatever office they held, he told them to give them the respect the office demanded. The same applies to apostles, prophets, and other ministries. We are to respect them for their service in the Lord, especially those who labor for our spiritual well-being (this speaks very heavily to pastors).

*For if a man think himself to be something, when he is nothing, he deceiveth himself. But let every man prove his own work and then shall he have rejoicing in himself alone, and not in another. (Galatians 6:3-4)*

Apostles are not to boast about their labors, for it leads to deception. Conversely, they are to rejoice before the Lord because of the reward He gives.

## Apostles and Pastors

The enemy is the author of confusion and division. If he can keep the leaders in the Church divided, they will not minister effectively in the Church. We have already addressed the fact that apostles are not to think more highly of themselves than they ought. However, since pastors usually have the oversight of local churches and assemblies, there is a need for understanding between apostles and pastors.

At the heart of the strife and tension between apostles and pastors is the need for control, blurred by personal insecurities. When a pastor has an apostle in his church, he must not allow insecurity and intimidation to grip his spirit. If so, he will perceive everything the apostle does as a challenge to his authority.

Conversely, the apostle should not try to handle situations reserved for the pastor of the Church. The pastor has the responsibility for the souls of the sheep. He also bears the responsibility for the spiritual oversight of the apostles that are in fellowship with the assembly.

Oftentimes, the enemy causes a war between pastors and apostles. The pastors feel intimidated by the manner in which God uses the apostles, and the apostles feel that the pastor is against them because of a persecution complex. The need for communication is vital.

Without communication, there will be confusion, and no one will benefit, but the kingdom of Satan. Pastors have to resist fighting apostles to feel like they are in control. Control is not the issue, but ministry. However, apostles have to learn to be subject to leadership if they expect to have fruitful ministries.

All ministries are needed in the Body of Christ. Pastors cannot devalue the ministries of apostles because they are under their ministries. Pastors need to understand that this ministry is foundational and is an asset to any ministry.

Conversely, apostles cannot feel that they are "above" pastors because of the authority and anointing upon their lives. Ministries are given to work together in peace. It is with this understanding that apostles and pastors have to work together in the local church or assembly.

**Apostles versus Prophets**

Another reoccurring trend in the Body of Christ is apostles trying to function as prophets and prophets trying to function as apostles without the anointing or call of the Lord.

Apostles will have to function sometimes in prophetic voices in the Body of Christ. However, this is not to be their area of concern. Their main job is to advance the Kingdom of God, not to be prophets.

Because some apostles have become deceived, thinking that they are all of the ministry gifts wrapped into one, they began to prophesy beyond the measure of their gifts. This turns into a soulish prophetic ministry, which usually ends up with the apostle thinking that he cannot ever be wrong.

The apostle then begins to prophesy for money and personal gain. Then, the apostle usually develops a following based upon his personality rather than the person of Christ. The result is then a deceived apostle with a following of beguiled souls.

Prophets also have to guard themselves against thinking that God is going to elevate them to the apostolic office. It is true that Paul was a prophet/teacher before entering into apostolic ministry. However, this was at the call of the Lord.

With some, God does use the prophetic office as training for the apostolic office. Many prophets, though, have taken it upon *themselves* to try to operate as apostles. They begin to start ministries and churches claiming apostolic authority and right. The result is a deceived prophet whose prophetic ministry is stifled by deception.

Though there are similarities between apostles and prophets, they must resist intruding on one another's offices based upon their own desires. In addition, apostles and prophets have to resist competing among themselves as to which office takes preeminence in the Church. The Word declares that He placed the apostles first. However, all ministries are equally important to the plan and purpose of God in the earth. No ministry is better, though functions differ.

Apostles and prophets have to learn how to relate to one another through the Spirit, balanced by humility and love. In order for the church to keep Apostles and Apostolic ministry in the proper perspective, misconceptions of this office have to be.

## Responding to Misconceptions

There are many false beliefs circulating about apostles and their ministries. We shall now explore some of the prevailing misconceptions surrounding the apostolic office.

## I. Paul is the standard for all apostles.

One mistake that Christian theologians have made is to make the ministry of Paul the standard for all apostles. Scholars infer that Paul is the barometer for all apostles because his ministry is highlighted more than others.

However, God operates in diversity even among those with the same ministry. Though Peter and Paul were apostles, Galatians informs us that they did not minister to the same group, or in the same manner.

> On the contrary, they saw that I had been entrusted with the task of preaching gospel to the Gentiles, just as Peter had been to the Jews. For God, who was at work in the ministry of Peter as an apostle to the Jews, was also at work in my ministry as addressed an

apostle to theGentiles. (Galatians 2:7-8 NIV)

**II. Not all apostles will do evangelistic work and will actively be involved.**

In the scriptures, we read of apostles like Peter, Paul, Barnabas, and Apollos who traveled frequently and ministered. However, other apostles were stationary like James and the other apostles located in Jerusalem. The scriptures give no indication that these men traveled extensively, but numerous accounts are given of these men sending emissaries to monitor the growth of the Church. Among those sent from them were Paul, Barnabas, Judas and Silas, Agabus and other prophets, and Peter.

*Then pleased it the apostles and elders, with the whole church, to send chosen men of their own company to Antioch with Paul and Barnabas; namely, Judas surnamed Barsabas, and Silas, chief men among the brethren. (Acts 15:22)*

### III. Not all apostles will start churches.

Because of the ministry of Paul and Barnabas, it has become the rule that apostles will start churches. James, who exercised oversight in Jerusalem, did not start the work there. Paul and Barnabas had to start churches in order to give the Gentiles an order for the worship of God. They went in areas where Christ was not preached. Therefore, they had to start churches and appoint leaders.

Please remember, a sign of the apostolic anointing is the starting of churches and organizations, but it is not mandatory. The scriptures give no indication that this is a necessary qualification to be an apostle.

If we hold to this belief, we would have to call every leader that has started a church, organization, or ministry, an apostle. We know that this is not true. The qualification for apostolic ministry is based upon godly attributes and power.

> *Truly the signs of an apostle were wrought among you in all patience, in signs, and wonders, and mighty deeds. (II Corinthians 12:12)*

## IV. An apostle is not an apostle over all.

Some immature apostles and leaders have promoted the doctrine that if someone is an apostle; they exercise apostolic authority over any church they choose. This is not true. An apostle is only an apostle where he is received as an apostle.

> *Yea, so have I strived to preach the gospel, not where Christ was named, lest I should*

> *build upon another man's foundation. (Romans 15:20)*
>
> *Am I not an apostle? am I not free? Have I not seen Jesus Christ our Lord? Are not ye my work in the Lord? If I be not an apostle unto others, yet doubtless I am you: for the seal of mine apostleship are ye in the Lord. (I Corinthians 9:1-2)*

Paul did not preach the gospel where any others had preached Christ, and he only exercised apostolic oversight over churches he established. He was given apostolic oversight over churches he did not start at their request.

> *For I would that ye knew what great conflict I have for you, and for them at Laodicea, and for as many as have not seen my face in the flesh; That their*

*hearts might be comforted, being knit together in love, and unto all riches of the full assurance of understanding, to the acknowledgement of the mystery of God, and of the Father, and of Christ. (Colossians 2:1-2)*

**V. Local churches do not need to be under an apostle's ministry.**

It is true that any church that receives an apostle or is under a true apostle's ministry will be greatly blessed. However, there were numerous churches in the apostle's day that was not under apostolic control. The church at Antioch was started after the saints fled persecution (Acts 11:19).

The elders at Jerusalem sent Paul and Barnabas to check on the work, not to take control. The Jerusalem apostles and elders did not replace the leadership with their own elders. They left the church in the hands of those who began it.

In addition, we find that at the church of Antioch, no apostles were named. Only prophets and teachers seemed to exercise rule and authority. We discover that these leaders were intricate in launching Paul and Barnabas into the apostolic ministry. Acts 13:1-3 states,

> Now there were in the church that was at Antioch certain prophets and teachers; as Barnabas, and Simeon that was called Niger, and Lucius of Cyrene, and Manaen, which had been brought up with Herod the tetrarch, and Saul. As they ministered to the Lord, and fasted, the Holy Ghost said, Separate me Barnabas and Saul for the work

*whereunto I have called them. And when they had fasted and prayed, and laid their hands on them, they sent them away.*

**VI. An apostle does not have to function in another ministry before operating in apostolic ministry.**

With the acceptance of apostles came this restriction: To operate in apostolic ministry, one must first operate in another one of the ministry offices. It is true that some apostles operated in other ministries before they became apostles, this was the case with Paul and Barnabas.

In Antioch, Paul (Saul) and Barnabas were listed among the prophets and teachers. There are apostles, today, who have operated for years as prophets, evangelists, and pastors before God released them into the greater work. God used the other offices as their training. It will enhance the apostolic ministry in them.

If someone can teach, evangelize, pastor, and be a prophet without operating in another ministry, the same holds true for the apostle. We read of men like James, Jude, and Apollos who were of note among the apostles without t having operated in another capacity in the Church. Timothy and Titus were under Paul's instruction and then they were released into apostolic ministry to the churches where he sent them.

## VII. Apostles are not exempt from accountability and Church authority. (I Timothy 5:20)

Apostles are not to be their own bosses. If they are heads of organizations, then they need to be in fellowship and accountability with other leaders. Also, if an apostle is not the overseer over a church but has ministry; he must be in fellowship with a local assembly or governing body as any other saint. Apostles are not above rebuke, correction, and discipline. Paul rebuked Peter when he was in error.

> *But when Peter was come to Antioch, I withstood him to the face, because he was to be blamed. For before that certain came from James, he did eat with the Gentiles: but when they were come, he withdrew and separated himself, fearing them which were of the circumcision. And the other Jews dissembled likewise with him; insomuch that Barnabas also was carried away with their dissimulation. But when I saw that they walked not uprightly according to the truth of the gospel, I said unto Peter before*

> *them all, If thou, being a Jew, livest after the manner of Gentiles, and not as do the Jews, why compellest thou the Gentiles to live as do the Jews? (Galatians 2:11-14)*

If someone is an apostle, and the pastor is not, the apostolic minister is not above the local leader. The pastor is his head and he must be submitted to him. Paul submitted his ministry to the leadership in Jerusalem for counsel.

> *And I went up by revelation and communicated unto them that gospel which I preach among the Gentiles, but privately to them which were of reputation, lest by any means I should run, or had run, in vain. (Galatians 2:2)*

Knowledge of the office the apostle is important to understanding the work of Christ in the Church. Illumination helps to develop an appreciation for this ministry and a desire to see it in operation along with the prophets, evangelists, pastors, and teachers.

-Chapter 6-
# What is Apostleship?

"I have an apostolic anointing." "I have been called as an apostle." "I am an apostle." These are expressions that are increasingly heard in the Body of Christ. Some believers are put off by them. Though some individuals who say this may be in error.

God has placed the apostolic gift in the Body of Christ. It is not only reserved for those who are apostles, but for any believer whom the Spirit will endow.

The apostolic grace is a widely misunderstood gift; so, many are still confused about its use, function, and purpose. In this chapter, we want to discover the fulness of the apostolic gift and ministry in the Body of Christ. The totality of apostolic ministry is described in one word: *apostleship.* It is a term used by Paul to describe his ministry.

> *By whom we have received grace and apostleship, for obedience to the faith among all nations, for his name. (Romans 1:5)*

However, apostleship is something that the Spirit will give to whom He will. The word *apostleship* means commission. There are individuals in the Body of Christ who are not apostles but have a commission from God. God operates in diversity. There are different aspects of apostleship demonstrated in the Body of Christ. There are levels to apostleship. As we discuss each, we will understand the purpose of apostleship in the Church.

**The Apostolic Gift**

In its simplest form, again, apostleship is a commission. There are individuals in the Body of Christ who have received a specific commission from the Lord. Individuals who receive such a commission share in the first level of apostleship. They have an apostolic gift.

The apostolic gift manifests in different ways. Ministers who have an apostolic gift will oftentimes start churches and religious organizations by the command of the Lord. They may not be apostles, but they will be sent to certain areas to pastor or start organizations whereby the Kingdom of God advances. However, after the church is planted and the organization established, the apostolic gift takes a 'back seat' to the calling on their lives.

In the laity, individuals who have an apostolic gift will start departments and auxiliaries in their churches. They will have vision to see the local assembly grow. They will be faithful members in service.

Aside from organizational skills and abilities, anyone who has an apostolic gift will, at times, exercise authority in the Spirit. They will also demonstrate the power of God. They will be spiritually sensitive men and women who have only a desire to please Christ.

**The Apostolic Anointing**

There are individuals in the Church who are not apostles, but there is a definite apostolic touch on their lives and ministries. These individuals are said to possess an apostolic anointing. This is the next level of apostleship. How does this differ from someone who has an apostolic gift? In simple terms, the person who has an apostolic gift will demonstrate apostolic grace and ability occasionally.

However, an individual with an apostolic anointing will demonstrate apostolic power, grace, and authority regularly as they minister to the Body of Christ. Possessing an apostolic anointing does not place one in the office of the apostle, but it does make them a part of the emerging apostolic company of believers.

The apostolic anointing is seen oftentimes in believers who are called to the five-fold ministry. They will operate in their respective offices while exercising apostolic power and authority. The apostolic anointing adds a depth and dimension to their ministries. In addition, one does not have to be called to a ministry office to possess an apostolic anointing (discussed earlier). These individuals are strategically placed in the Body of Christ that all may be partakers of the apostolic ministry.

*Individuals who possess an apostolic anointing will manifest the revelation and power*

***of the Spirit consistently.*** They will have encounters with the Lord frequently. This may be in dreams and visions or in visitations of the Holy Spirit. In addition, they will be able to help others grow in their relationship with the Lord.

Some will function like missionaries (sent ones) between churches. They will travel from assembly to assembly, strengthening pastors and leadership through their service. The next manifestation of the apostolic spirit is, of course, **The Apostolic Office,** which is the focus of this book. We shall go on to the next level of the apostolic ministry in the Church.

**The Apostolic Spirit**

The greatest expression of apostleship is not in the apostolic gift, the apostolic anointing, or the ministry of the apostle. It is in the apostolic spirit. The early Church was effective because they appreciated and accepted the ministry of the apostles. As a result, great grace and power rested upon the thousands of believers in Jerusalem.

> *And they continued stedfastly in the apostles' doctrine and fellowship, and in breaking of bread, and in prayers. And fear came upon every soul: and many wonders and signs were done by the apostles. And all that believed were together, and had all things common; And sold their possessions and goods, and parted them to all men, as every man had need. And they, continuing daily with one accord in the temple, and breaking bread from house to house, did eat their meat with gladness and singleness of heart, Praising God, and having favour with all the people. And the*

*Lord added to the church daily such as should be saved. (Acts 2:42-47)*

The early Church demonstrated the apostolic spirit. This is the highest level of apostleship. Jesus' words to the apostles illustrate the manifestation of the apostolic spirit.

*And he said unto them, Go ye into all the world, and preach the gospel to every creature. He that believeth and is baptized shall be saved; but he that believeth not shall be damned. (Mark 16:15-16)*

In the Gospels, Jesus gives a charge to the apostles before He ascended. It is understood that the charge given to them is one that the Church is to fulfill corporately.

*Go ye therefore, and teach all nations, baptizing them in the name of the Father, and of the Son, and of the Holy*

*Ghost: Teaching them to observe all things whatsoever I have commanded you: and, lo, I am with you alway, even unto the end of the world. Amen. (Matthew 28:19-20)*

The Church is sent to the world to represent Christ. The apostolic spirit represents the Church's apostleship to the world. How does this affect the local assembly? When an assembly embraces the apostolic spirit, three things are evident. They are the same things that were evident in the early Church.

1. **Unity** – When the apostolic spirit is manifested in an assembly, every believer will operate in love and support of one another. The sign of a true follower of Christ is love. Love, in turn, produces unity.

*By this shall all men know that ye are my*

> *disciples, if ye have love one to another. (John 13:35)*

Since God and Christ are love, the apostolic spirit compels believers to work together in unity. The unity produced through the apostolic spirit sets the stage for the manifestation of power in the Church.

2. **Power** – The assembly walking under an apostolic spirit will be a place of healing, deliverance, and salvation. The miraculous will be seen daily in the life of that church. The least to the greatest among the people will demonstrate the power of God in healing the sick, casting out of devils, and effective evangelism.

> *And these signs shall follow them that believe; In my name shall they cast out devils; they shall speak with new tongues; They shall take up serpents; and if they*

*drink any deadly thing, it shall not hurt them; they shall lay hands on the sick, and they shall recover. (Mark 16:17-18)*

3. **Expansion of the Kingdom of God** – After unity and power, the church flowing in the apostolic spirit will cause expansion in the Kingdom. The assembly will grow, not because of other believers coming to fellowship. It will grow because souls will be added daily to the Kingdom because of the power and love expressed. In turn, the assembly will be a force in its city, county, and state because of the apostolic spirit.

*And the Lord added to the church daily such as should be saved. (Acts 2:47b)*

The apostolic spirit is something that every fellowship of believers should seek for. The early Church had it and the Lord prospered them. If we possess it, we will see the miraculous of the

Books of Acts today. In addition, the Kingdom of God will advance. Now that we have discussed the different aspects of apostleship, we have created an **Apostolic Ascension** diagram showing the different levels in apostleship.

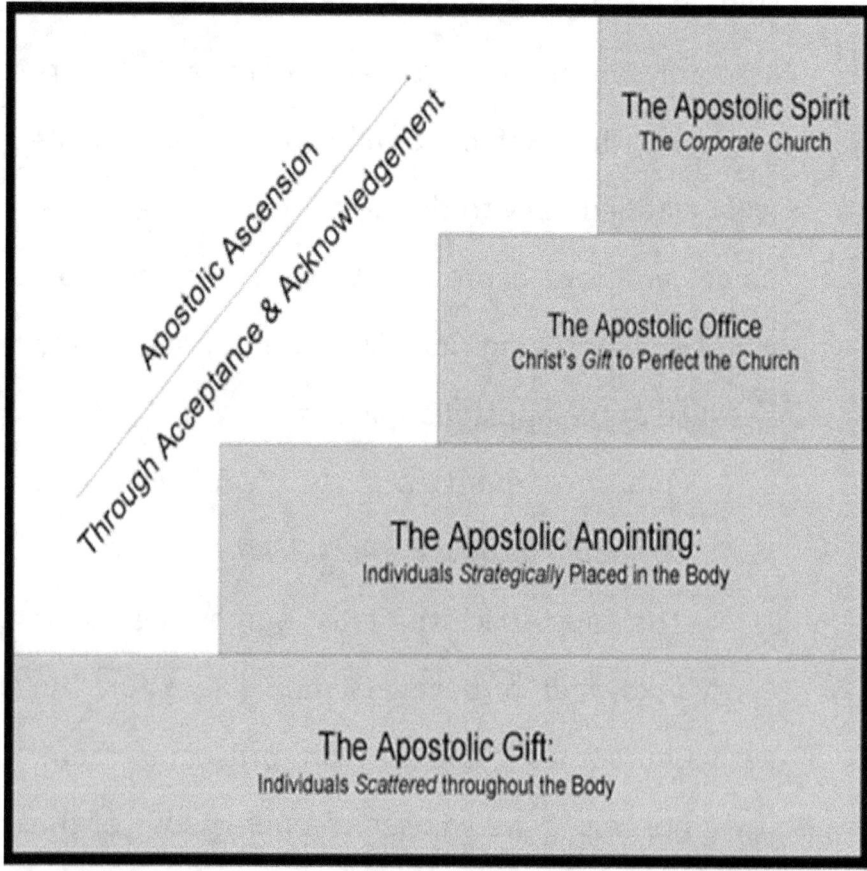

The apostolic progression from the apostolic gift to the apostolic spirit is comparable to a flight of steps. The only way to go higher, one has to climb the steps. If the Church appreciates the apostolic gift, apostolic anointing, and apostolic office, we will experience the apostolic spirit in our day. The apostolic spirit will only manifest as the apostleship of the believers and apostles is accepted and received. The apostolic spirit is something the entire Church is to possess.

The illustration of the steps provides the basis for a general truth concerning the apostolic. The Church is supposed to be an apostolic Church. It is to reflect Christ's nature and power. The Church cannot become an apostolic Church without the ministry of the apostles and the apostolic anointing.

As the Church embraces (accepts and acknowledges) each manifestation of the apostolic, it moves a step closer to becoming apostolic corporately, culminating with the Church fulfilling its commission given by Christ to the apostles.

**Guidelines for Judging the Apostolic**

One of the major facets of understanding apostleship is to discern when something is not apostolic. Judging the apostolic can be a tough task at times. Nevertheless, there are guidelines to help us as we strive to receive those with this gift and anointing.

We need the apostolic in the Church, but some of us have lost faith in the apostolic gift and ministry. If you are unsure as to what and who is apostolic, there are certain questions you can ask yourself.

We must understand that God is the giver of the apostolic grace. We do not need to be afraid, but discerning. Even if we have heard or seen individuals misrepresent the apostolic office and gift, we should not allow the enemy to steal a blessing from us. God may be trying to even birth an apostolic gift in you or send someone with this anointing for your benefit.

**Is the individual humble?** Those with an apostolic calling and gift will be humble. They will know that without God, they can do nothing. They will consistently turn the people's attention to Christ and not themselves.

> *But God forbid that I should glory, save in the cross of our Lord Jesus Christ, by whom the world is crucified unto me, and I unto the world. (Galatians 6:14)*

Conversely, do not be quick to say someone

does not have this gift or anointing because of character flaws. Apostles and apostolic individuals grow in grace and character as other believers.

**Is their doctrine sound and full of wisdom?** Those with an apostolic gift (ministers or not) will have a clear understanding of the scriptures. They will be able to present the word of God with clarity. They will continue to develop their doctrine because they respect God and His word. They desire that all understand God's truth through the scriptures.

On the other hand, there are apostolic individuals who have a valid gift, but they are in the middle of God's process of perfecting. They still may be on the potter's wheel. Some may try to operate in this anointing and gift before time. This may contribute to elementary or erroneous doctrine.

**Do they follow leadership?** Apostolic individuals will respect and follow leadership. Christ came in submission to the Father. Apostolic individuals will support leadership. They know that this is pleasing to Christ.

Individuals who find it hard to follow leadership may not have sat at the foot of Christ. One sign of an apostolic call is that they follow Christ. To follow Christ is to follow His example. He ministered in submission to the Father. The apostolic individual will minister in subjection to leadership.

**Is there a manifestation of authority and power in the Spirit of God?** Part of the apostolic call is the working of the miraculous power of God. Any individual claiming an apostolic gift or anointing should show some level of giftedness by the Spirit and results in ministering. There should be testimonies of salvation, healing, and deliverance from others concerning them.

**Is there confirmation of the apostolic call or gift?** God is not the author of confusion. He does not work against Himself. He will not give a gift or calling without providing some form of confirmation in the Body. Even if your gift is not specifically stated, there will be a recognition of the grace that is upon your life.

However, if an individual is claiming the apostolic office, there will be confirmation (usually by elders and apostles) of the ministry. Shun away from individuals claiming an apostolic call and no one else knows about it. Usually, these individuals are self-willed. They demonstrate little power. Oftentimes, they are not faithful or accountable to anyone.

-Chapter 7-
# False Apostles

**THE BELIEVER'S GUIDE TO THE APOSTOLIC MINISTRY** — A Comprehensive Study of the Apostolic Ministry in the Church

There is still much to be learned about the apostolic office. However, understanding comes with responsibility. The Church has to stand against deception. The scriptures are clear that the number of false ministers will increase as the end of this age approaches.

Not every individual preaching in the name of the Lord is His servant. The enemy seeks to destroy the work of God in the earth through imitation. Therefore, the enemy sets his false ministers in the Church to undermine the work of God's chosen vessels. False ministers are here, but the saints are not to be afraid of falling into deception. False ministers provide a service to the Church.

How?

*For there must be also heresies among you, that they which are approved may be made manifest among you. (I Corinthians 11:19)*

When Paul used the word heresies, he was speaking of divisions and those that caused them. False ministers seek to keep the Church in perpetual dissension and division. Their ministries put enmity between believers with the intent to create a following for themselves. The answer to "How do false ministers provide a service to the Church?" seems non-existent. However, the statement of Paul provides a simple explanation.

False ministers help us to recognize true ministers of God. Paul said that there must be heresies (and those that cause them) among you so that those who are approved (right, true, anointed, etc.) might be made visible. The ministries of false ministers demonstrate to the Church the improper way to minister. Therefore, when true ministry is in operation, it can be received without fear.

**Recognizing False Ministers**

We cannot end our discussion of apostles without discussing false apostles. Before examining false apostles exclusively, it is imperative that we are able to recognize the characteristics of any false minister (or layman). Jesus gave this warning concerning false ministers.

> Beware of false prophets, which come to you in sheep's clothing, but inwardly they are ravening wolves. Ye shall know them by their fruits. Do men gather grapes of thorns, or figs of thistles? Even so every good tree bringeth forth good fruit; but a corrupt tree bringeth forth evil fruit. A good tree cannot bring forth evil fruit, neither can

*a corrupt tree bring forth good fruit. Every tree that bringeth not forth good fruit is hewn down and cast into the fire. Wherefore by their fruits ye shall know them. (Matthew 7:15-20)*

One true way to recognize false ministers is by the fruit that they bear. Fruit refers to their lifestyles and not their ministries. Moreover, not everyone that is false calls himself an apostle or prophet. Though false apostles exist, there are also false evangelists, pastors, and teachers. Regardless of the title that a false minister has, he (or she) will exhibit the following characteristics.

**They preach that godliness is gain.** Godliness to false ministers means prosperity and healing. They seldom teach against sin. They promote serving God for what you can get.

> *If any man teach otherwise, and consent not to wholesome words, even the words of our Lord Jesus Christ, and to the doctrine which is according to godliness; He is proud, knowing nothing, but doting about questions and strifes of words, whereof cometh envy, strife, railings, evil surmisings, perverse disputings of men of corrupt minds, and destitute of the truth, supposing that gain is godliness: from such withdraw thyself. (I Timothy 6:3-5)*

They only teach that you belong to God and should have the best. They promote the concept that God only wants you blessed, without declaring that God also wants character, integrity, and holiness in His people. Their doctrine focuses on the miraculous work of God and His blessings, exclusively. They promote God's blessing, rather than God and His Christ. They teach individuals how to prosper in God without living for Him.

**They were once servants of God.** Many false ministers have genuine conversion experiences. They entered ministry by the call of God. However, consistent rebellion, sin, pride, and greed caused them to error from the truth.

> *For if after they have escaped the pollutions of the world through the knowledge of the Lord and Saviour Jesus Christ, they are again entangled therein, and overcome, the latter end is worse with them than the beginning. For it had been better for them not to have known the way of righteousness, than, after they have known it, to turn from the holy commandment delivered unto them. But it is happened unto them*

*according to the true proverb, the dog is turned to his own vomit again; and the sow that was washed to her wallowing in the mire. (II Peter 2:20-22)*

Peter wrote that false ministers did escape the pollutions of the world by Christ. However, they returned to their sins and filthy ways. Consequently, Peter added, they are worse than they were before their initial conversion. It serves as a warning to every minister. If the love of money, pride, and sin are not rejected, the road to becoming an enemy of God becomes inevitable.

**Recognizing False Apostles**

False apostles will demonstrate the same behavior as other false ministers. However, there will be certain traits that readily visible in false prophetic ministers.

**They minister for money.** False apostles will always include money in their ministry. No matter the topic or subject, it will end up on money. They will twist scriptures to manipulate the people into giving to them. Remember:

***NO APOSTLE OF SCRIPTURE EVER PREACHED FOR MONEY.***

They will tell you to give in order to "seal" the prophetic words that they speak. We should give to ministers that have blessed us, but it should never be by their request. We can bless those that have blessed us spiritually.

In the scriptures, they would bless the apostle because of the spiritual impartation. They gave because they wanted to, not because the apostle demanded it.

**They operate in false authority.** False apostles do not operate in godly authority. They establish their own authority in the Body of Christ. They disguise their wickedness by first appearing as true apostles.

*For such are false apostles, deceitful workers, transforming themselves into the apostles of Christ. And no marvel; for Satan himself is transformed into an angel of light. Therefore it is no great thing if his ministers also be transformed as the ministers of righteousness; whose end shall be according to their works. (II Corinthians 11:13-15)*

Paul stated that those who are false would resemble those who are true. However, once they have gained some respect, they will attack other leaders. The false apostles and leaders of Paul's day tried to defame him and establish their own authority in the churches. False apostles use this tactic today. Through the defamation of others, they exalt their personal ministries.

**They twist the scriptures.** Another tactic used is misinterpretation of scripture to establish authority. They find scriptures that refer to apostolic authority and claim it for themselves. They scare believers into thinking that because they are apostles, they are superior to others.

True apostles will be humble. They will not promote their personal ministries. The authority that they operate in is backed by the power of God and recognized in the Church.

**They operate in counterfeit gifts.** False apostles minister with the wrong motives. Therefore, the Spirit of God withdraws Himself from their ministries. Since false apostles do not recognize the withdrawal of God, they strive to operate in gifts to validate the ministry. They begin to rely on their own human spirit and help from demonic influence to appear spiritual. This happened to King Saul.

> *But the Spirit of the Lord departed from Saul, and an evil spirit from the Lord troubled him. (I Samuel 16:14)*
>
> *And it came to pass on the morrow, that the evil spirit from God came upon Saul, and he prophesied in the midst of the house: and David played with his hand, as at other times: and there was a javelin in Saul's hand. (I Samuel 18:10)*

Because of Saul's continual rebellion, the Spirit of God departed from him. An evil spirit replaced God's Spirit. When the evil spirit came upon him, he prophesied. His prophecy came from the wrong source. This eventually happens to false apostles. The Holy Spirit leaves and they use demonic influence to still function.

**They prophesy lies from their imaginations.** False apostles will pretend to have a valid prophetic gift. They will make up lofty prophetic utterances. They will seem very spiritual, but oftentimes vague in content.

> *I have heard what the prophets said,* that prophesy lies in my name, saying, I have dreamed, I have dreamed. How long shall this be in the heart of the prophets that prophesy lies? yea, they are prophets of the deceit of their own heart. (Jeremiah 23:25-26)

They will give prophecies based upon someone's outer appearance and expression. In addition, they prophesy their own desires. Conversely, because a prophetic word may seem vague, it does not mean it is not from the Lord. The Lord may speak a word in part that the hearer would be drawn into seeking the Lord for clarity.

**They possess a controlling spirit.** False apostles will use manipulation to gain followers. Once people begin to follow them, they scare the individuals into staying. They tell individuals that if they leave, God will not be pleased and the like.

In addition, the apostle will try to control the people's personal lives. By using false authority, they will tell people who they can marry and where to work. False apostles operate in a similar fashion to cult leaders.

Though false apostles and ministers exist, believers are not to walk in fear. However, Christians have to be able to learn to recognize false ministers. In addition, the presence of false ministers should give believers a greater appreciation for godly leaders and ministries within the Church.

# -Book 3-
# The Apostolic Revolution:

Exploring the Apostolic Restoration and Reformation

Apostles and apostolic ministry are important to the furtherance of the Kingdom of God and the Church. But, some have become vulnerable to deception and error. Many apostles have abused their ministries and authority. Therefore, the Lord is going to send an apostolic paradigm shift in the midst of the Church. In the first book of this series, we will show the events that led to the primary apostolic revolution in the early Church. We will discuss how there was a need for a replacement in the early apostles which was the prerequisite for the outpouring of the Spirit and formation and foundation of the establishment of the New Testament faith and early disciples.

# Preface

Apostles and apostolic ministry are important to the furtherance of the Kingdom of God and the Church. It is my prayer that the information presented in this work will prepare believers for the reformation that will occur in the demonstration of the apostolic ministry.

Numerous works have been produced which highlight the ministry of the apostle. However, the information in this book will bring believers into a greater understanding of the shift coming to apostles and apostolic ministry

Roderick Levi Evans

# Introduction

As the disciples waited for the promise of the Faithe; that is, the baptism of the Holy Ghost, they cast lots to discover who would replace Judas. When the qualified candidate was selected, they continued in prayer.

After this, the Holy Spirit came upon those gathered in the upper room, and they instantly became powerful witnesses of the Resurrection. Souls were converted and the new converts were confirmed in the faith.  The Apostolic Ministry Revival Series was developed to reveal how God is bringing a restoration and revival to apostles and apostolic ministry for an end time expansion of the Kingdom of God and establishing of believers in the faith.

**THE BELIEVER'S GUIDE TO THE APOSTOLIC MINISTRY** — A Comprehensive Study of the Apostolic Ministry in the Church

## In this publication:

Controversy over the gifts and ministries of the Spirit has abounded for centuries. Various scholars have taught that there was a cessation of the gifts and ministries. More specifically, they affirm that the ministry of the Apostle is no longer in operation nor valid. However, in recent years, a resurgence of the operation and demonstration of this ministry occurred.

Traditional and Non-traditional churches, alike, have experienced the visitation of God through the Holy Spirit. Since the emergence and acceptance of the ministries and gifts of the Holy Spirit, various authors have written concerning this phenomenon.

In spite of this, many in the Church, presently, do not understand the functions and operations of, namely, the office of the Apostle.

Even in organizations and denominations that consider this ministry valid today, comprehension is oftentimes elementary.

Where there is no clear understanding, individuals become vulnerable to deception and error. Many apostles have abused their ministries and authority. Therefore, the Lord is going to send a reformation in the midst of the Church. It is designed to bring purity again to the apostolic office. Not only in the execution of this ministry, but also in the perspective for which it is received.

In the first book of this series, we will show the events that led to the primary apostolic revolution in the early Church. We will discuss how there was a need for a replacement in the early apostles which was the prerequisite for the outpouring of the Spirit and formation and foundation of the establishment of the New Testament faith and early disciples.

**THE BELIEVER'S GUIDE TO THE APOSTOLIC MINISTRY** | A Comprehensive Study of the Apostolic Ministry in the Church

**THE BELIEVER'S GUIDE TO THE APOSTOLIC MINISTRY**

A Comprehensive Study of the Apostolic Ministry in the Church

-Chapter 1-
# The Apostolic Restoration

"Elias truly shall first come and restore all things (Matthew 17:11)." Jesus' words revealed God's wisdom in restoration. Throughout history, when God wanted restoration of fellowship with man, He would send an individual to prepare the way.

God spoke to Noah to warn of His impending destruction of the world. No man heard him and only he and his family were saved.

## The Ancestral Demonstrations

After man multiplied upon the face of the earth, God chose Abraham to be the Father of many nations through faith in Him. At the appointed time of Israel's exodus from Egypt, God sent Moses as the deliverer and giver of the Law. All of these men were used to restore the proper worship of God.

Israel's history reflects God's desire for continual fellowship with mankind. However, when they broke covenant and fellowship, God used the prophets to call for repentance and restoration. One of the most notable prophets of Jewish history is Elijah (Elias, in some translations).

When Israel (through Ahab and Jezebel's evil reign) strayed away from the Lord, God sent Elijah to challenge the wickedness and restore Israel to God. His words on Mount Carmel reveal his mission.

> *And Elijah came unto all the people, and and said, How long halt ye between two opinions? If the Lord be God, follow him: but if Baal, then follow him. And the people answered him not a word. (I Kings 18:21)*

Because of the character and power demonstrated in Elijah's ministry, he became the symbol of repentance and restoration. Malachi revealed this truth in his prophetic messages.

> *Behold, I will send you Elijah the prophet before the coming of the great and dreadful day of the Lord. And he shall turn the heart of the fathers to the children, and the heart of the children to their fathers, lest I come and smite the earth with a curse. (Malachi 4:5-6)*

Before the Messiah came, Malachi revealed that Elijah would come first. His job was to restore fathers and children. Spiritually, he would turn the hearts of men unto God. We discover that God did not send the first Elijah back, but He sent a man who came in the spirit and likeness of Elijah; that is, John, the Baptist.

> *In those days came John the Baptist, preaching in the wilderness of Judaea, And saying, Repent ye: for the kingdom of heaven is at hand. (Matthew 3:1-2)*

In his time, John was a modern day 'Elijah' challenging the established religious system of the day. His mission was to bring restoration. He restored man's perspective and worship of God through baptism unto repentance. This, in turn, prepared man for the One who was to come.

When He came, the fullness of the Father and His purposes would be revealed. We see demonstrated in Abraham, Elijah, and John ancestral demonstrations of apostolic ministry.

Today, we find that God is bringing a full restoration of the ministries and gifts of the Spirit in the Church. In recent decades, the prophetic ministry became very prominent. Like Elijah, today's true prophets challenged the hypocrisy and covetousness of this generation.

John (in Elijah's spirit) prepared the world for the Apostle of the Faith. Thus, the prophetic ministry corporately functioned as the "Elijah," which was to come, preparing the way for the apostles.

*And Jesus answered and said unto them, Elias truly shall first come, and restore all things. (Matthew 17:11)*

**The Apostolic Restored**

The apostolic paradigm shift begins with a restoration. In recent years, three dimensions of the apostolic have been restored. The first is the sending forth and the acceptance of modern-day apostles. God released individuals into the Kingdom of God who without a doubt could be classified as apostles. Again, the corporate ministry of the prophets prepared the way.

The second is the work of the modern-day apostles. The apostles that came forth restored understanding of the apostolic office, ministry, and function. Without this, immature and false apostles would continue to damage the credibility of those who are mature and true; subsequently, frustrating God's plan for the apostolic ministry presently.

The third dimension of the apostolic restoration is the required character of apostles. This results in a restoration of appreciation and respect for apostles and their ministries. It is within this third area of restoration that we discover the heart of the apostolic paradigm shift.

The paradigm shift will not only take place in the acceptance and work of apostles, but in the character reflected in those in this ministry. Jesus is called the Apostle and High Priest of the Faith.

> *Wherefore, holy brethren, partakers of the heavenly calling, consider the Apostle and High Priest of our profession, Christ Jesus. (Hebrews 3:6)*

He set the standard for apostles and apostolic ministry. When we understand how he functioned as an apostle, we can discover why an apostolic paradigm shift is necessary. Jesus is the true apostolic representative.

**THE BELIEVER'S GUIDE TO THE APOSTOLIC MINISTRY**   A Comprehensive Study of the Apostolic Ministry in the Church

-Chapter 2-

# The Apostolic Representative

The apostolic reformation comes to produce apostles who will mirror the apostolic ministry of the Christ. The standard set by Christ went beyond fulfilling God's plan. He showed us that we were to fulfill His plan with character. Three things characterized Jesus' apostolic ministry and character.

**Obedience**

As the Apostle, Jesus walked in obedience to the Father. He was not self-willed or stubborn. He did not rebel against the commission given to Him. Hebrews declared Jesus' understanding of His ministry.

> *Then said I, Lo, I come (in the volume of the book it is written of me,) to do thy will, O God. (Hebrews 10:7)*

Jesus came only to do the will of God. He did not have any other agenda. His ministry exhibited total obedience to God. Hear the words of His testimony,

> For I came down from heaven, not to do *mine own will, but the will of him that sent me. (John 6:38)*

If obedience is not the foundation of the apostle's ministry, it will be defective and ineffective. If Jesus walked in obedience to the Father and He was Lord of all, the apostle has to have the same mind. Jesus' obedience included His ministry and lifestyle. He was blameless and without sin.

The apostle's obedience has to reflect this. After preaching, teaching, prophesying, evangelizing, and ministering, the apostle has to walk in obedience to God's standards for holy and righteous living, which involves personality traits also.

## Faithfulness

` As the apostolic representative, Jesus demonstrated the faithfulness required in an apostle. After revealing Christ as the Apostle of the Faith, the writer of Hebrews revealed His faithfulness.

> *...consider the Apostle and High Priest of our profession, Christ Jesus; who was faithful to him that appointed him, as also Moses was faithful in all his house. (Hebrews 3:1b-2)*

Jesus added faithfulness to obedience. He did not quit or shun His responsibilities because of adversity. He tolerated endless criticism and rejection. He also endured the pain and agony of the cross. He did not allow His trials, test, and troubles to hinder Him.

Every apostle has to remain faithful to the calling. The apostolic ministry brings controversy and contention. Faithfulness sustains the apostle in times of struggle. Jesus remained faithful to the Father. The modern-day apostle has to remain faithful in spite of consistent rejection, and misunderstanding. Apostles today should reflect the faithfulness of Christ.

**Love**

Jesus' obedience and faithfulness in His earthly ministry was tempered by love. Christ's motivation in ministry was love. He remained obedient and faithful because He loved God and He loved mankind. He fulfilled the greatest of the commandments.

> *Master, which is the great commandment in the law? Jesus said unto him, Thou shalt love the Lord thy God with all thy heart, and with all thy soul, and with all thy mind. This is the first and great commandment.*

*And the second is like unto it, Thou shalt love thy neighbour as thyself. (Matthew 22:36-39)*

Because of love, Jesus remained focused on His mission. The modern-day apostle's foundation for ministry has to be love. In my book, *The Apostle Question (pgs. 55-56)*, the character traits of the apostle revealed through love were examined. Love governed Christ's actions and it has to rule in the apostolic minister today. Here is the excerpt,

> *"Love has to be the foundation of the apostle's ministry. God is love. Christ demonstrated His love for us through His obedience to God and His death on the cross.*
>
> *God's involvement with men is always through His love. His correction and*

*discipline is rooted in love. The apostle has to be the express image of God. No matter what his ministry entails, it must be done through love.*

*Charity suffereth long, and is kind; charity envieth not; charity vaunteth not itself, is not puffed up, doth not behave itself unseemly, seeketh not her own, is not easily provoked, thinketh no evil; rejoiceth not in iniquity, but rejoiceth in the truth; Beareth all things, believeth all things, hopeth all things, and endureth all things. (I Corinthians 13:4-7)*

*The apostle has to have an everlasting love for God, the Church, and his family. If he rebukes, corrects, admonishes, teaches, warns, and prays, love has to be the source. The apostle's demonstration of love must match Paul's description of love as recorded in I Corinthians 13."*

Jesus is the true apostolic representative. His life and ministry stands as the model of valid apostolic ministry. If apostles today possess the obedience, faithfulness, and love of Christ, they will become effective vessels in the present-day reformation.

**Authentic Apostolic Ministry**

When authentic apostles and apostolic ministry function properly, God's plan and purpose for the Church will be realized. The apostolic restoration, reformation, and ensuing paradigm shift finds its definition within the biblical account of the disciples in the upper room.

After Jesus' ascension, the disciples waited for the outpouring of the Holy Spirit. The events in the upper room before Pentecost clearly demonstrate the totality of the apostolic reformation and paradigm shift presently taking place (Acts 1:15-26). While in the upper room, we can identify four apostolic personalities. Understanding of these will clarify the apostolic paradigm shift of today. The first two will discussed in this book, and the following book of this series.

*Judas – The Apostolic Rejected*

> *For it is written in the book of Psalms, Let his habitation be desolate, and let no man dwell therein: and his bishoprick let another take. (Acts 1:20)*

*Peter – The Apostolic Respected*

> *And in those days Peter stood up in the midst of the disciples... (Acts 1:15)*

*Matthias – The Apostolic Paradigm shift*

> *And they gave forth their lots; and the lot*

> *fell upon Matthias; and he was numbered with the eleven apostles. (Acts 1:26)*

### Joseph – The Apostolic Representation

> *And they appointed two, Joseph called Barsabas, who was surnamed Justus, and Matthias. (Acts 1:23)*

The manifestation of these apostolic personalities produced a reformation of the worship of God and the expansion of the Kingdom of God.

The present-day apostolic reformation will do the same. The failure of Judas as one of the apostles of the Lamb set the stage for the apostolic reformation of his day. When we understand the apostolic that is rejected, we can embrace the paradigm shift and reformation that is coming.

-Chapter 3-

# The Apostolic Refused

**THE BELIEVER'S GUIDE TO THE APOSTOLIC MINISTRY** — A Comprehensive Study of the Apostolic Ministry in the Church

Though Jesus is the perfect representative of apostolic ministry, there is an individual who embodies the refused apostolic ministry; that is, Judas Iscariot. Jesus chose him as an apostle and disciple. The Gospels record,

> *And when it was day, he called unto him his disciples: and of them he chose twelve, whom also he named apostles; Simon, (whom he also named Peter,) and Andrew his brother, James and John, Philip and Bartholomew, Matthew and Thomas, James the son of Alphaeus, and Simon called Zelotes, And Judas the brother of James, and Judas Iscariot... (Luke 6:13-16)*

Judas had a valid calling accompanied with the power of God. He received power along with the other disciples for ministry.

> *And when he had called unto him his twelve*

*disciples, he gave them power against unclean spirits, to cast them out, and to heal all manner of sickness and all manner of disease. (Matthew10:1)*

However, Judas rejected his calling and position; his apostleship was revoked. Through consideration of Judas' beliefs, betrayal, and bleak end, we can identify the apostolic that God has **refused** today.

**Judas' Beliefs**

What led to Judas' betrayal? The scriptures are unclear as to the exact reason. However, whatever governed Judas' belief system contributed to his betrayal of Christ. There are numerous theories suggested to explain his treachery. Three are commonly argued: religious fervor, personal greed, and demonic deception.

*Religious Fervor*

The first theory suggested for Judas' betrayal is religious fervor. Some historians suggest that Judas was a member of a radical Jewish sect called the Zealots. This sect desired to see the Jewish people freed from Roman control.

They dreamt of a day when Israel would be returned to the glory and power that it once possessed. However, the Zealots had a "by any means necessary" attitude. They promoted a violent, physical overthrow of the Roman government.

Since Jesus did not come to release them from Roman control but the control of sin, some propose that Judas betrayed Him because He did not help to support the cause.

It is believed that Judas saw Jesus as a

traitor to His people because His zeal to overthrow Rome did not match that of the Zealot sect. Consequently, he sold him to the Pharisees.

*Religious Fervor Today*

As apostles surface, there are some who fit into this category. They forget that they are ambassadors for Christ and begin to follow their own agendas. Numerous apostles have become concerned with the organization of the Church and the institution of larger buildings, institutions, and community services, while neglecting the advancement of the Kingdom of God, which can only be done through the conversion of souls.

There are apostles today who are on the road to betraying Christ because they became consumed with the work of the Lord and left Him out. Other apostles become ambassadors for the apostolic ministry rather than Christ.

They began to preach that apostles are the cornerstone of the Church rather than Christ. They become so consumed with trying to establish the role of apostolic ministry in the Church that they forget to demonstrate it. They began to preach apostles and not Christ.

Whenever religious activities and ministries become the central focus of an apostle, they become spiritual Zealots for the wrong cause. If Judas was a Zealot, his personal agenda caused him to betray Christ for his own cause. and

**Judas' Betrayal**

Apostles today are experiencing refusal from the Father because they are working for their advancement and not the Kingdom of God.

*Personal Greed*

The second commonly proposed theory is that Judas was greedy. It has also been suggested that Judas became disillusioned with Christ because it did not lead him into personal wealth. Before Jesus called Judas, it is reported that he was a thief. However, in service to the Lord, he was responsible for the finances.

> *This he said (Judas), not that he cared for the poor; but because he was a thief, and had the bag, and bare what was put therein. (John 12:6, Parenthesis mine)*

From this, it is argued that Judas expected the fame of Christ to bring him fortune. From the scriptures, we understand that Christ did not live as a king, but He lived modestly (oftentimes depending on the hospitality of others) in ministry. Judas, again, may have been disappointed and saw Jesus' betrayal as a way to make some money.

*Personal Greed Today*

Numerous ministers, especially apostles are candidates for refusal because of personal greed. The apostolic that is refused is one that values money over ministry. There are apostles whose apostleship will be or has been revoked because of greed. They use their God-given authority and position to get wealthy. They use clichés to get money from the Lord's people.

Judas was greedy. His greed was not under control though he walked with Jesus. This is why he had a problem with the woman anointing Jesus' feet with oil. He wanted to get the money in his possession. It is believed that this act pushed him over the edge. The gospels record that immediately following this incident that he conspired to betray Him.

> *She hath done what she could: she is come aforehand to anoint my body to the burying. Verily I say unto you, Wheresoever this gospel shall be preached throughout the whole world, this also that she hath done shall be spoken of for a memorial of her. And Judas Iscariot, one of the twelve, went unto the chief priests, to betray him unto them. And when they heard it, they were glad, and promised to give him money. And he sought how he might conveniently betray him. (Mark 14:8-11)*

Apostles who are candidates for refusal deter others from giving to please Christ to giving to only 'bless' the apostle of God. Judas was refused and apostles today will face refusal. Greed will definitely lead to betrayal.

## Demonic Deception

The third theory is that Judas submitted to demonically induced deception. His suspected religious fervor and personal greed had little impact on his betrayal. Support for this comes from scriptures also,

> *And supper being ended, the devil having now put into the heart of Judas Iscariot, Simon's son, to betray him. (John 13: 2)*

The scriptures are clear that Judas' betrayal was strengthened by demonic influence. He had previously discussed arrangements with the Pharisees for Jesus' betrayal, but the devil made sure that he went through with it.

This demonstrates that the adversary capitalized on the wickedness already present within Judas. This gave him no defense against demonic influence.

*Demonic Deception Today*

Judas allowed the devil to deceive him into betrayal. Though he walked with Jesus, he did not allow His teachings to change his heart though he participated in His work.

> *...lest that by any means, when I have preached to others, I myself should be a castaway. (I Corinthians 9:27b)*

There are apostles today who operate in ministry with success. Yet, they have not allowed the ministry they have preached to change them inwardly. They leave themselves open to demonic influence. Apostles who are self-willed, stubborn, arrogant, and prideful are subject to demonic delusion. In this state, they become candidates for refusal.

Regardless of one's personal opinion concerning Judas' beliefs, it is clear that any apostles who hold to them will be or have been refused of God. Judas serves as a warning to all: Do not allow ungodly belief systems to govern ministerial activities! Judas' betrayal was solidified with a kiss.

Apostles have to guard against blessing Christ with their mouths and betraying them with their activities. Revocation of apostleship will be inevitable. Judas did not enjoy the money that he received for the betrayal.

Those who lose their apostleship will discover that the reward for betrayal was not worth it. Paul addressed this truth in this manner,

*For many walk, of whom I have told you often, and now tell you even weeping, that they are the enemies of the cross of Christ. (Philippians 3:18-19)*

-Chapter 4-
# The Apostolic Rejected

**THE BELIEVER'S GUIDE TO THE APOSTOLIC MINISTRY** — A Comprehensive Study of the Apostolic Ministry in the Church

Rejected apostles will experience shame and sorrow as God fills their positions with faithful servants.

**Judas' Bleak End**

Judas' betrayal of Christ did not end with his restoration. His story concluded with suicide. Judas' demise is recalled in complimenting accounts of his last moments.

> *And he cast down the pieces of silver in the temple, and departed, and went and hanged himself. (Matthew 27:5)*
>
> *Now this man purchased a field with the reward of iniquity; and falling headlong, he burst asunder in the midst, and all his bowels gushed out. (Acts 1:18)*

Judas ended his own life. Rejected apostles, likewise, commit spiritual suicide. Peter's corresponding account of what happened to Judas reveals what happens to an apostle on the road to rejection. All can recognize these traits. Three things occurred in Judas' end.

*Purchased a Field with the Reward of Iniquity*

Rejected apostles and apostolic ministers engage in ungodly practices for personal gain. The betrayal money Judas received was used to purchase a field. Rejected apostolic ministries will acquire positions, authority, wealth, promotions, and favor through the exercise of ungodly character traits.

Be mindful of apostles and apostolic individuals who equate godliness with gain. This mindset is popular among those who are on the way to rejection.

*Perverse disputings of men of corrupt minds, and destitute of the truth, supposing that gain is godliness: from such withdraw thyself. (I Timothy 6:5)*

Though God delights in the prosperity of His saints, any apostles whose message focuses solely on this truth set themselves up for a fall.

*Fell Headlong*

After hanging himself, Judas fell headlong to the ground. In other words, he fell headfirst. Falling headlong represents apostles who become heady and high-minded; that is, prideful. Pride has subdued countless ministries throughout the ages. To help Paul resist pride, God gave him a thorn in the flesh.

Apostles on the path to rejection are full of pride. They, like Judas, fall headfirst. The scriptures declare that pride paves the way for destruction.

> *Pride goeth before destruction, and an haughty spirit before a fall. (Proverbs 16: 18)*

Beware of apostles and apostolic individuals who promote themselves and their ministries only. Their ministries consist of comparing themselves with others and exalting their personal accomplishments. Their sermons consist of testimonies of their greatness rather than the declaration of His greatness. Rejected apostles subject themselves to the same fate as Judas and will fall headfirst as he did.

### He burst Asunder & Bowels Gushed Out

Judas fell headfirst. Yet, when he hit the ground, his stomach was split in two. Consequently, his intestines (bowels) spilled out. Rejected apostles depart from following God to pursuing the lusts of the flesh. In the scriptures, those who became false made a god out of their bellies.

> *Whose end is destruction, whose God is their belly, and whose glory is in their shame, who mind earthly things. (Philippians 3:19)*

Rejected apostles will be disciplined and judged according to their evil desires. The bowels spilling represents God exposing those whom he has rejected. The hidden desires and motives will be revealed to all.

**The Case for Rejection**

Some reading this will think that God will not revoke an individual's ministry. There is precedent for such an act in the scriptures. If God does not change and Christ is the same yesterday, today, and forever, we can safely conclude that continual rebellion in the New ministry. King Saul rebelled and refused to follow the Lord repeatedly. God rejected him.

> *For rebellion is as the sin of witchcraft, and stubbornness is as iniquity and idolatry. Because thou hast rejected the word of the Lord, he hath also rejected thee from being king. (I Samuel 15:23)*

He revoked the kingdom from him and his seed. In spite of this, Samuel continued to pray for him. However, God did not receive his prayer for the rebellious and self-willed king.

> *And the Lord said unto Samuel, How long wilt thou mourn for Saul, seeing I have rejected him from reigning over Israel? (I Samuel 16:1a)*

King Saul's persistent rebellion and refusal to follow the Lord wholeheartedly resulted in God's rejection of him. Saul was king without the presence and endorsement of the Lord. Though he continued to reign for some years, he was still rejected.

There are apostolic ministers, today, who are rejected but allowed to maintain their positions. Like Saul, God no longer endorses them. Rather than repent, they are satisfied to keep a title and position. If continual rebellion resulted in Saul's rejection, continual rebellion will result in an apostle's rejection.

-Chapter 5-
# The Apostolic Respected

**THE BELIEVER'S GUIDE TO
THE APOSTOLIC MINISTRY**  A Comprehensive Study of the Apostolic Ministry in the Church

Because many apostles have subjected themselves to the pursuit of this world's goods, fortune, and fame, they have walked in the way of Judas, the rejected apostle. They have contributed to the increase of the rejected apostolic. In turn, God is sending forth apostles in these days who will walk in the obedience, faithfulness, and love of Christ.

The apostolic reformation will be ushered in with the assistance of established apostolic ministers. In the upper room, Peter recognized Judas' rejection and the need for a replacement.

*And in those days Peter stood up in the midst of the disciples, and said, (the number of names together were about an hundred and twenty,) Men and brethren, this scripture must needs have been fulfilled, which the Holy Ghost by the mouth of David spake before concerning Judas, which was guide to them that took Jesus. (Acts 1:15-16)*

In order for the reformation to come into fruition, established apostles are responsible to bring forward the new company of apostles God is sending forth. Peter represents the apostolic that is respected. He recognized that there was someone else needed to stand with them in ministry as apostles of the Lamb. Apostles who want to take part in what God is doing have to follow in Peter's example.

**Peter's Insight**

In the upper room, the disciples gathered to wait upon the reception of the Holy Ghost. It was in this atmosphere that Peter demonstrated insight into the purposes of God. He understood that Judas' actions fulfilled prophecy. And again, there was a need to fill his position based upon that which was revealed in the scriptures.

Peter exhibited apostolic insight. He was knowledgeable of the scriptures and he knew how to apply them to the present situation. Because of this, he became the catalyst for the restoration and reformation of the apostolic ministry originally purposed by Christ, which consisted of twelve apostles.

Apostolic Insight Today

Apostles today need spiritual insight into the upcoming move of God. Like Peter, they need to understand the scriptures and their impact on what is occurring today. Mature apostles will see the need for true apostolic ministers and assist in their entrance into kingdom work.

### Peter's Integrity

Along with spiritual insight, Peter displayed integrity. Judas' rejection left a vacancy that needed to be filled. Peter did not try to reserve a special place for himself and the other apostles.

He demonstrated selflessness in apostolic ministry. He wanted others whom the Lord had chosen to come forward in ministry. He was concerned with the work of the kingdom and not personal glory. In response to this, he put forth an inquiry to the other disciples. He wanted to find someone who would be able to replace Judas.

*For it is written in the book of Psalms, Let his habitation be desolate, andlet no man dwell therein: and his bishoprick let another take. Wherefore of thes men which have companied with us all the time that the Lord*

*Jesus went in and out among us? (Acts 1:20-21)*

## Apostolic Integrity Today

Apostles today have to walk in the integrity of Peter. Some apostles feel that they are the only true apostles left and feel that no one else can stand with them in ministry. This was not Peter's view.

He knew that in order for the work to be accomplished, others were needed to help. Apostles today need this mindset. Apostles have the responsibility to facilitate new ministries into the Body.

> *But Barnabas took him, and brought him to the apostles, and declared unto them how he had seen the Lord in the way, and that he had spoken to him, and how he had preached boldly at Damascus in the name of*

*Jesus. (Acts 9:27)*

Today's established apostles have to do for apostolic ministers what Barnabas did for Paul. Since there was controversy surrounding Paul's conversion, Barnabas (a respected disciple) presented him to the Church. Apostles have to guard against trying to protect a position or title and allow God to use them to accomplish His purposes.

**Peter's Invocation**

Following Peter's insight, integrity, and inquiry concerning the need for the rejected apostle's replacement, he and the disciples prayed. They prayed for God to reveal *His* choice.

> *And they prayed, and said, Thou, Lord, which knowest the hearts of all men, shew whether of these two thou hast chosen,*

> *That he may take part of this ministry and apostleship... (Acts 1:24-25a)*

Peter's insight produced action. They prayed until God gave revelation of Judas' replacement. He and the others knew that the one chosen to stand with them needed to have God's endorsement. Though they look for suitable candidates, the Lord gave the final endorsement.

## Apostolic Invocation Today

The respected apostolic of today and the established apostles have to give themselves to prayer to effectuate the apostolic reformation that is occurring. Peter's revelation led to invocation. Those apostles who have understanding of the apostolic transition have to be willing to labor in intercessory prayer until those whom God has chosen, take their rightful positions.

Because Peter recognized the vacancy and was a catalyst for filling the void, it led to a paradigm shift in apostolic ministry and in the Church. The same, which, is happening today.

In the next book, we will explore the events in the upper room, the outpouring of the Sprit, and the first apostolic revolution, which sets the precedence for the apostolic paradigm shift occurring presently.

**THE BELIEVER'S GUIDE TO THE APOSTOLIC MINISTRY**  A Comprehensive Study of the Apostolic Ministry in the Church

# -Book 4-
# The Apostolic Paradigm Shift:

Examining the Coming Reformation of Apostles and Apostolic Ministry

Apostles and apostolic ministry are important to the furtherance of the Kingdom of God and the Church. But, some have become vulnerable to deception and error. Many apostles have abused their ministries and authority. Therefore, the Lord is going to send an apostolic paradigm shift in the midst of the Church. It is designed to bring purity again to the apostolic office. Not only in the execution of this ministry, but also in the perspective for which it is received. In this book, we will explain the apostolic paradigm shift God is sending in the Church.

**THE BELIEVER'S GUIDE TO THE APOSTOLIC MINISTRY** — A Comprehensive Study of the Apostolic Ministry in the Church

# Preface

Apostles and apostolic ministry are important to the furtherance of the Kingdom of God and the Church. It is my prayer that the information presented in this work will prepare believers for the reformation that will occur in the demonstration of the apostolic ministry.

Numerous works have been produced which highlight the ministry of the apostle. However, the information in this book will bring believers into a greater understanding of the shift coming to apostles and apostolic ministry

Roderick Levi Evans

**THE BELIEVER'S GUIDE TO THE APOSTOLIC MINISTRY** — A Comprehensive Study of the Apostolic Ministry in the Church

# Introduction

As the disciples waited for the promise of the Faithe; that is, the baptism of the Holy Ghost, they cast lots to discover who would replace Judas. When the qualified candidate was selected, they continued in prayer.

After this, the Holy Spirit came upon those gathered in the upper room, and they instantly became powerful witnesses of the Resurrection. Souls were converted and the new converts were confirmed in the faith. The Apostolic Ministry Revival Series was developed to demonstrate how God is bringing a restoration and revival to apostles and apostolic ministry for an end time expansion of the Kingdom of God and establishing of believers in the faith.

THE BELIEVER'S GUIDE TO
THE APOSTOLIC MINISTRY    A Comprehensive Study of the Apostolic Ministry in the Church

**THE BELIEVER'S GUIDE TO THE APOSTOLIC MINISTRY**  A Comprehensive Study of the Apostolic Ministry in the Church

-Chapter 1-

# The Apostolic Paradigm Shift

**THE BELIEVER'S GUIDE TO THE APOSTOLIC MINISTRY**

A Comprehensive Study of the Apostolic Ministry in the Church

In the first book, we discussed how the apostolic paradigm shift began with a restoration of the acceptance, work, and character of the apostolic ministry through an apostolic revolution. After this restoration, an apostolic rejection proceeded from the Lord against disobedient and self-willed apostles throughout the centuries. This led to the need for reformation.

We also discussed how that established apostles should intercede and prepare the way for the apostolic paradigm shift to take place. One must understand that the apostolic paradigm unfolds as a company of apostles comes forward in the Kingdom of God.

Continuing our examination of the events in the upper room from the first book of this series, we discover that the choosing of Matthias (to stand with the other eleven) reflects the present-day apostolic transition.

As we consider the man, Matthias, we will understand the fullness of God's present move It is within this apostolic personality that we find the heart of the apostolic paradigm shift. Peter requested that the disciples present find men who met certain qualifications to replace Judas.

> *Wherefore of these men which have companied with us all the time that the Lord Jesus went in and out among us, Beginning from the baptism of John, unto that same day that he was taken up from us, must one be ordained to be a witness with us of his resurrection. (Acts 1:21-22)*

When they had looked among them, they found two men, which met all of these qualifications: Matthias and Joseph.

*And they appointed two, Joseph called Barsabas, who was surnamed Justus, and Matthias. (Acts 1:23)*

After prayer, the lot fell upon Matthias as the Lord's choice for apostleship. When we examine more closely the calling and ordination to the apostolic ministry, we discover how the apostolic paradigm shift will operate.

**Matthias: The Chosen Apostle**

Matthias was chosen by the Lord to stand with the apostles. He did not exalt or endorse himself. Yet, the Lord made clear that he was His choice. The disciples could recognize the signs of apostleship, but a clear approval from the Lord had to accompany it.

From this, we discover that the company of apostles that are emerging will have the Lord's seal upon them. Like Matthias, God has reserved them until this present time to place them in position.

> *So the last shall be first, and the first last: for many be called, but few chosen. (Matthew 20:16)*

The apostles coming will not be stubborn, self-willed, or prideful, but in *humility*, will they receive the Lord's calling and walk therein.

## Matthias: The Silent Apostle

We have no record of Matthias in any of the Gospels. We discover that one of the qualifications for apostleship was that he had to have been with Jesus from His baptism until His ascension. Matthias remained *faithful* to Christ without recognition or fame.

The apostles ushering in the apostolic paradigm walk in the way of Matthias. They have been *faithful* to the Lord in secret.

*Moreover it is required in stewards, that a man be found faithful. (I Corinthians 4: 2)*

They have maintained godly lifestyles and have spent time developing their relationship with Him. They did not do it for a position or ministry, but because they were dedicated to the Lord.

Matthias followed the Lord for His entire earthly ministry without any position. This prepared him for the future ministry. The emerging apostles have served because they were committed to the Lord. In turn, He will reveal them to the world as He did Matthias.

### Matthias: The Processed Apostle

Matthias walked with Christ from the baptism of John. Though he was not a part of the inner twelve, he, too, had to leave all and follow Christ. He had to be present in the places where Christ traveled and ministered.

Undoubtedly, he experienced some difficulties and hardships when he made a decision to follow Christ. Thus, he was prepared to endure the hardships that come with apostolic ministry.

The apostles of the apostolic paradigm shift are individuals who have gone through the Lord's breaking and molding process. Matthias had to witness Jesus' baptism from John.

John's baptism was one to repentance. This demonstrates that the emerging apostles will have forsaken unrighteous and ungodly lifestyles and ambitions. They are apostles who are willing to call men to repentance as they walk in repentance from dead works.

The coming apostles will be individuals whom the Lord has allowed to suffer great rejection, persecution, failures, and setbacks to ensure that they will remain humble in service. They will appreciate the apostolic call, bringing honor to God and respect for the office.

> *But the God of all grace, who hath called us unto his eternal glory by Christ Jesus, after that ye have suffered a while, make you perfect, stablish, strengthen, settle you. (I Peter 5:10)*

## Matthias: The Prepared Apostle

Matthias was present; according to all of the qualifications presented by Peter, the whole time Jesus went in and out among them.

Therefore, he received teaching and instructions from Christ. He may have been among the seventy that were sent out by Christ.

> *After these things the Lord appointed other seventy also, and sent them two and two before his face into every city and place, whither he himself would come. (Luke 10: 1)*

If this is true, which is highly probable, Matthias and the others were not sent out without instructions for service and an understanding of the kingdom.

The apostolic individuals coming from obscurity are taught of the Lord. They will minister with sound doctrine and understanding. Many of them will have a similar testimony to Paul's. He declared that he received a revelation of the Gospel from Christ.

> *But I certify you, brethren, that the gospel which was preached of me is not after man. For I neither received it of man, neither was I taught it, but by the revelation of Jesus Christ. (Galatians 1:11-12)*

This means that these apostles will not preach from the wisdom of men. They have sat at the Lord's feet and received the necessary tools for ministry. They stand prepared to declare fully the mysteries of the Kingdom of God.

They will only present that which is clearly revealed through the scriptures and revelation of the Spirit. They will not preach about themselves or ministries, but only things pertaining to the Kingdom of God and His Christ.

Their ministries in the word will bring men back into the purity of the faith. They will present Christ as Lord. Their preaching and teaching will not be laced with covetousness and hypocrisy. They will lead men and women to the risen Christ. Their message will prepare men for the coming of the Lord. Remember, all New Testament ministry will point to the second coming of Christ.

**Matthias: The Committed Apostle**

Matthias also demonstrated a commitment to the Lord and to the brethren. Peter stated the apostle who replaced Judas had to have companied with them all the time while Christ was in the earth. Not only did Matthias follow the Lord, but also he had fellowship with the other disciples. This revealed his connection with other followers of the Lord.

The apostolic paradigm shift will reveal apostles who have a love for the Church. They will not be lone rangers. They will promote unity and love among the Body of Christ.

Some apostles use apostolic ministry to divide the Church and to gain a following. The coming apostles will demonstrate a love for the brethren. Their commitment to the Church will mirror the sentiment of Paul when he stated,

> *Behold, the third time I am ready to come to you; and I will not be burdensome to you: for I seek not yours, but you: for the children ought not to lay up for the parents, but the parents for the children. And I will very gladly spend and be spent for you... (II Corinthians 12:14-15a)*

Paul revealed his love for the saints at Corinth. He was willing to give all that he had for their success in the kingdom of God. The apostolic paradigm shift will produce apostles who are selfless and willing to lay down their lives (ministries, time, prayer, and gifts) for the Body of Christ.

**Matthias: The Seer-Apostle**

Another qualification listed by Peter was that the individual had to have seen Jesus ascend back into heaven (solidifying the witness of the resurrection). Matthias was present when the Lord gave final instruction and teachings ending with His reception into heaven. He had an eyewitness experience of the Lord in His glory. For this cause, he, like the others, can be called 'seer-apostles.'

The term 'seer-apostle' reveals the spiritual insight and revelation of the emerging apostolic company. First, they will see the Lord for who He is. Their perception and presentation of Christ will be genuine in presentation and application. They have a revelation of Christ. Second, they will have spiritual insight into the plans and purposes of God in the earth.

Thirdly, they will have a proper perception of who they are and their place in the Lord's service. Finally, the revelatory gifts of the Spirit will manifest in them consistently and accurately. Many of the coming apostles will have ministries similar to John, the Beloved. They will have a pronounced prophetic ministry complimenting their primary roles as apostles.

The ordination of Matthias marked a change in the apostolic ministry of the day. It marked the beginning of change. Matthias is the personality of the apostolic paradigm shift. His example will be emulated in the apostles of the apostolic paradigm shift. The apostolic paradigm shift will produce apostles of character and integrity, which sets the stage for a move of God in the earth.

Before examining the effects of the present and ensuing apostolic paradigm shift, we want to examine another personality in the apostolic paradigm shift. Another man possessed the necessary qualifications to replace Judas as Matthias, but he was not chosen to take part in the ministry of the apostles: the disciple named Joseph.

-Chapter 2-

# The Apostolic Representation

Matthias reflects the heart of the apostolic paradigm shift. His replacement of Judas reveals God's work of removing apostles who have rejected His leadership. In turn, He is filling their positions with apostles of character and integrity.

The upper room events, however, reveal that another individual stood out among the brethren as a candidate for apostleship. Again, it was the disciple named Joseph.

> *And they appointed two, Joseph called Barsabas, who was surnamed Justus, and Matthias. (Acts 1:23, Emphasis mine)*

When I considered this, I asked God for wisdom. If Matthias represented the company of apostles coming forth, what did the disciples' recommendation of Joseph represent?

The wisdom of God revealed that Joseph represented a company of apostolic individuals who would emerge throughout the Body of Christ. These individuals would not be apostles, but they (like Joseph) will meet the qualifications for apostolic ministry.

This company of believers will possess an apostolic anointing upon their lives, which enhances their service to the Lord. Joseph becomes then the personality of the coming apostolic representation in the Body of Christ.

Since he met the same qualifications as Matthias, an examination of his example is necessary to understand how the apostolic representation will operate in the Church.

**Joseph: The Called Apostolic**

The apostles chose Joseph as a candidate for apostleship. We discover that the Lord had chosen Matthias. We have no record of Joseph feeling rejected or causing division among the disciples. He accepted that the Lord had not called him as an apostle of the Lamb.

From this, we discover that the company of apostolic individuals will be comfortable in their service to the Lord. They will not seek fame, fortune, position, or title. They, like Joseph, will continue to serve the Lord without titles. They understand that God has given them a measure in the apostolic and will not operate in a manner reserved for apostles only. They understand Jesus' words,

> *...for there be many called, but few chosen. (Matthew 20:16)*

The apostolic representation coming will not be stubborn, self-willed, or prideful, but in *humility*, will they work supporting those who stand on the front lines of ministry.

**Joseph: The Secret Apostolic**

We have no record of Joseph, like Matthias, in any of the Gospels. Again, one of the qualifications for apostleship was that he had to have been with Jesus from His baptism until His ascension. Joseph remained *faithful* to Christ without recognition or fame.

The apostolic individuals have been *faithful* to the Lord in secret. However, their work in the Body will bless countless others.

*Moreover, it is required in stewards, that a man be found faithful. (I Corinthians 4:2)*

They have maintained Christ-centered lifestyles and have spent time developing their relationships with Him. They did not do it for a position or title, but because they were committed to Christ. Joseph followed the Lord throughout His ministry without any position.

This revealed his personal dedication to Christ. The emerging apostolic individuals have served because they were committed to the Lord. In turn, He will anoint and use them greatly in the Church and world.

**Joseph: The Processed Apostolic**

Joseph walked with Christ from the baptism of John. Though he was not a part of the inner twelve, he, too, had to leave all and follow Christ. He had to be present in the many places where Christ traveled and ministered. Undoubtedly, he experienced some difficulties and hardships when he decided to follow the Savior. He prepared himself to endure the hardships that came with service to Christ.

The people of the apostolic representation have experienced the Lord's breaking and molding process. Joseph witnessed Jesus' baptism from John. John's baptism was one to repentance. This demonstrates that the emerging apostolic representation will have allowed the teachings of Christ to break down unrighteous and ungodly lifestyles and ambitions. They are willing to challenge other believers in their walks with the Lord and compel men to repent of their sins to follow Jesus.

The coming apostolic individuals will be individuals whom the Lord has allowed to suffer great rejection, persecution, failures, and setbacks. They will have testimonies of God's deliverance from grievous trials and tests. They, too, will appreciate the apostolic anointing upon their lives, bringing honor to God.

*But the God of all grace, who hath called us Unto his eternal glory by Christ Jesus, after*

> *that ye have suffered a while, make you perfect, stablish, strengthen, settle you. (I Peter 5:10)*

## Joseph: The Prepared Apostolic

Joseph, like Matthias, was present; according to the qualifications presented by Peter, the whole time Jesus went in and out among them. Therefore, he received teaching and instructions from Christ. He also may have been among the seventy that were sent out by Christ.

> *After these things the Lord appointed other seventy also, and sent them two and two before his face into every city and place, whither he himself would come. (Luke 10:1)*

If this is true, which is highly probable, Matthias, Joseph, and the others were not sent without instructions for service and an understanding of the kingdom. The apostolic individuals coming from obscurity are also taught of the Lord. They will minister with sound doctrine and understanding. Many of them will have a similar testimony to Paul's. He declared that he received a revelation of the Gospel from Christ.

> *But I certify you, brethren, that the gospel which was preached of me is not after man. For I neither received it of man, neither was I taught it, but by the revelation of Jesus Christ. (Galatians 1:11-12)*

This means that these apostolic individuals will know how to rightly interpret and explain the scriptures. They have sat at the Lord's feet and received for Him. They stand prepared to fully declare the Gospel of the Kingdom of

God.

They will communicate that which is clearly revealed through the scriptures and revelation of the Spirit. They will not promote themselves or falsehood, but only things pertaining to the Kingdom of God and His Christ.

Their presentation of the word will help to bring people back into the purity of the faith. They will present Christ as Lord. Their doctrine will be solid, not tainted with philosophy and vanity. They will lead men and women to the risen Christ. They will prepare the hearts of men for Christ's coming.

## Joseph: The Committed Apostolic

Joseph also demonstrated a commitment to the Lord and to the brethren. Peter stated the one who replaced Judas had to have companied with them all the time while Christ was in the earth. Not only did Joseph follow the Lord, but also he had fellowship with the other disciples, like Matthias. This revealed his connection with the other followers of the Lord.

The apostolic paradigm shift reveals apostolic individuals who have a love for their brothers and sisters in the Lord. They will not be selfish and reclusive. They will promote unity and love among the Body of Christ.

The coming apostolic representation will demonstrate a love for the Church. The apostolic representation will produce individuals who are selfless and willing to lay down their lives (ministries, time, prayer, finances, service, and gifts) for the brethren.

**Joseph: The Prophetic Apostolic**

The final qualification listed by Peter was

that the individual had to have seen Jesus ascend back into heaven (solidifying the witness of the resurrection). Joseph was present when the Lord gave final instruction and teachings ending with Him reception into heaven. He had an eyewitness experience of the Lord in His glory. Because of this, we discover that Joseph represents an apostolic representation with a prophetic touch.

The term prophetic reveals the spiritual insight and revelation of the emerging apostolic individuals. First, they will see the Lord for who He is. Their perception and presentation of Christ will be genuine in presentation and application. They have a revelation of Christ. Second, they will have spiritual insight into the plans and purposes of God in the earth.

Thirdly, they will have a proper perception of who they are and their place in the Lord's service. Finally, the revelatory gifts of the Spirit will manifest in them consistently and accurately. Many of those included in the apostolic representation will be like the daughters of Philip.

The daughters had recognized prophetic gifts, though they were not called prophets (some translations try to identify them as prophets, yet, most manuscripts only suggest that they prophesied only). Those in the apostolic representation will have valid prophetic gifts complimenting the apostolic anointing.

The disciples' recognition of Joseph's qualifications reveals the level of service and commitment those in the apostolic representation will possess. The apostolic paradigm shift will make its greatest impact upon the Church and the world as the apostolic individuals arise and stand to serve along with the apostles.

**THE BELIEVER'S GUIDE TO THE APOSTOLIC MINISTRY** | A Comprehensive Study of the Apostolic Ministry in the Church

-Chapter 3-

# The Apostolic Expression

For many years, prophets and other ministers have predicted the coming of a revival that will have global implications. These prophecies reveal that revivals will happen in many places around the world simultaneously. It will mark one of the Lord's final calls to repentance before the end of all things.

Though we have seen some notable revivals take place in recent decades, none seemed to match the Spirit's revelation of the revivals to come. There is still an end-time outpouring of the Spirit to come.

> *Repent ye therefore, and be converted, that your sins may be blotted out, when the times of refreshing shall come from the presence of the Lord. (Acts 3:19)*

## The Great Outpouring

After Matthias was ordained to stand with

the other apostles, something extraordinary happened.

> *And they gave forth their lots; and the lot fell upon Matthias; and he was numbered with the eleven apostles. (Acts 1:26)*

Shortly afterwards, the next event recorded was the outpouring of the Holy Spirit. The promised Spirit did not come until after the apostolic was restored. This reveals that the apostolic paradigm shift marks the beginning of the fulfillment of the modern-day prophecies of great revival. This is what is demonstrated from the events in the upper room.

> *And suddenly there came a sound from heaven as of a rushing mighty wind, and it filled all the house where they were sitting. And there appeared unto them cloven tongues like as of fire, and it sat upon each*

*of them. And they were all filled with the Holy Ghost, and began to speak with other tongues, as the Spirit gave them utterance. (Acts 2:2-4)*

## The Great Revelation

The outpouring of the Holy Spirit did not only signify the birth of the Church, but it ushered in a time when the revelation of God would abound in those that served him. When Peter stood to address the crowd, he told them what was the major by-product of the Spirit's outpouring.

*But this is that which was spoken by the prophet Joel; And it shall come to pass in the last days, saith God, I will pour out of my Spirit upon all flesh: and your sons and your daughters shall prophesy, and your young men shall see visions, and your old men shall dream dreams: And on my servants and on my handmaidens I will pour out in those days of my Spirit; and they shall prophesy. (Acts 2:16-18)*

The major result of the Spirit's outpouring was revelation; namely, prophetic utterances, dreams, and visions. If the apostolic paradigm shift of today will prepare the way for an outpouring, then we can safely conclude that there will be increase in the supernatural revelation of God and Jesus in the Church. Prophecy, dreams, visions, and the like will be in abundance to empower the Church for service.

-Chapter 4-

# The Apostolic Administration

This chapter is entitled the apostolic revelation. This does not refer to revelation from apostolic individuals, but it refers to the Church's corporate apostolic administration which reveals Christ to the world.

**The Great Testimony**

The outpouring of the Spirit and prophetic revelation makes this possible. The man that talked with John on Patmos reveals this truth when he states,

> ... for the testimony of Jesus is the spirit of prophecy. (Revelation 19:10)

The Holy Spirit comes with the spirit of prophecy. The Church needs the prophetic revelation of the Spirit to give the proper testimony of Jesus. It is through the spirit of prophecy that the apostolic commission is fulfilled.

*Go ye therefore, and teach all nations, baptizing them in the name of the Father, and of the Son, and of the Holy Ghost: Teaching them to observe all things whatsoever I have commanded you: and, lo, I am with you always, even unto the end of the world. Amen. (Matthew 28:19-20)*

## The Great Commission

The apostolic revelation that is produced by the apostolic paradigm shift propels the Church into success with the four-fold administration of Great Commission. The commission should produce four distinct phenomena:

I. An increase in evangelism
II. An expansion of the kingdom of God
III. Mature disciples
IV. Greater faith of the church

Increased Evangelism (Go ye...)

The apostolic paradigm shift will propel the Church into greater evangelistic efforts. Revivals, in recent decades, have been reduced to spiritual pep rallies. A return to evangelistic efforts with signs and wonders following will become common again. The ministry of the apostles and apostolic individuals will help the Church to walk in its former glory and power.

*And they went forth, and preached every where, the Lord working with them... (Mark 16:20)*

In turn, ministers and believers everywhere will begin to stand up as witnesses of Christ and His resurrection.

*Expansion of the Kingdom of God (Baptizing them...)*

The apostolic paradigm shift comes to

expand the kingdom of God, not to promote apostles and apostolic individuals. Their placement in the Body of Christ is to increase the effectiveness of the Church as it fulfills Christ's commission.

After the Spirit's outpouring, the apostles preached Christ. Moreover, the disciples preached Christ. This resulted in the salvation of many.

> *Praising God, and having favor with all the people. And the Lord added to the church daily such as should be* saved. (Acts 2:47)

The number of converts grew daily. This will be seen today as the apostolic paradigm shift unfolds.

*Mature Disciples (Teaching them...)*

In Jesus' commission to the disciples, there

was a charge to teach men what He commanded. The apostolic company of the apostolic paradigm shift will bring clarity to the mysteries of Christ. Like Paul, they will teach others what Christ has taught them.

> *And they continued steadfastly in the apostles' doctrine and fellowship, and in breaking of bread, and in prayers. (Acts 2:42)*

This results in mature disciples functioning in the Church. The apostolic paradigm shift will produce believers who not only will teach the commands of Christ but walk in those things that are presented.

Greater Faith in the Church (I am with thee always)

To conclude His charge, Jesus gave the promise of His abiding presence with the disciples.

This was to produce faith in them as they went out into a hostile world. In the face of opposition and persecution, they could maintain their resolve to be witnesses of Christ.

> *Behold, I send you forth as sheep in the midst of wolves: be ye therefore wise as serpents, and harmless as doves. (Matthew 10:16)*

Jesus' promise also was to inspire faith in the disciples to expect His supernatural power to accompany them as they ministered in His name. They were to be assured that signs would follow them.

> *And these signs shall follow them that believe; In my name shall they cast out devils; they shall speak with new tongues; They shall take up serpents; and if they drink any deadly thing, it shall not hurt*

*them; they shall lay hands on the sick, and they shall recover. (Mark 16:20)*

The effects of the apostolic paradigm shift will be seen in bold witnessing for Christ. In addition, an increase of the power and demonstration of the Holy Spirit will manifest. It is within the Great Commission that the apostolic revelation (the Church's revelation and its presentation of Christ) will be fully realized.

Before ending our explanation of the apostolic paradigm shift, we have to address its direct impact on the Body of Christ in particular.

**THE BELIEVER'S GUIDE TO THE APOSTOLIC MINISTRY**  A Comprehensive Study of the Apostolic Ministry in the Church

-Chapter 5-
# The Apostolic Reformation

**THE BELIEVER'S GUIDE TO THE APOSTOLIC MINISTRY** — A Comprehensive Study of the Apostolic Ministry in the Church

The coming apostolic paradigm shift will affect the Church in various ways. We have established that it will bring hidden apostles and apostolic individuals to the light for Kingdom work. Their work in the Church will set the stage for the end-time outpouring of the Holy Spirit.

This, in turn, will increase the effectiveness of the Church in fulfilling the Great Commission. Yet, there is one final task that the apostolic paradigm shift will perform. It will create an apostolic reformation in the general life of the Church.

The apostolic reformation in the Church will cause the modern-day Church to operate like the early Church. When apostles and apostolic individuals are in place, the authority and anointing of the Church increases. If we understand the apostolic paradigm shift and embrace the apostolic reformation, we will see the days of Acts repeated presently. The reformation will be seen in three areas:

**Reformation of Love**

When the apostolic reformation takes place, every believer will operate in love and support of one another. The sign of a true follower of Christ is love. Love, in turn, produces unity.

> *By this shall all men know that ye are my disciples, if ye have love one to another. (John 13:35)*

Since God and Christ are love, the apostolic spirit compels believers to work together in unity. Churches and organizations that are divided over non-essential doctrines will repent and come together.

## Reformation of the Miraculous

As the Church embraces the apostolic reformation, there will be an increase in healing, deliverance, and salvation. The miraculous will be common in the life of the Church. The least to the greatest among the people will demonstrate the power of God in healing the sick, casting out of devils, and effective evangelism.

> *And these signs shall follow them that believe; In my name shall they cast out devils; they shall speak with new tongues; They shall take up serpents; and if they drink any deadly thing, it shall not hurt them; they shall lay hands on the sick, and they shall recover. (Mark 16:17-18)*

## Reformation of Disciples

The apostolic reformation will cause

multiplication in the number of believers and disciples. There is a growing trend of individuals being religious in church without a conversion experience. They are church attendees but not disciples.

The apostolic reformation will cause those in the Church to go beyond religion into discipleship. The Church will grow, not because of religious people, but because souls are added who will be true followers of Christ. In turn, local assemblies will have great impact in their cities, counties, and states because of the apostolic reformation.

*And the Lord added to the church daily such as should be saved. (Acts 2:47b)*

The apostolic reformation prepares the possessed great power and authority. The apostolic reformation will cause the modern

Church to function as they did. If we embrace it, we will see the miraculous of the Books of Acts today. In addition, the Kingdom of God will advance.

The apostolic paradigm shift and reformation is upon us. Let us embrace what the Lord is doing in the Church today. In doing so, the Church's authority, anointing, glory, and power will be evident unto all men.

Closing Prayer...

> That the God of our Lord Jesus Christ, the Father of glory, may give unto you the spirit of wisdom and revelation in the knowledge of him: The eyes of your understanding being enlightened; that ye may know what is the hope of his calling, and what the riches of the glory of his inheritance in the saints, And what is the exceeding greatness

*of his power to us-ward who believe, according to the working of his mighty power, Which he wrought in Christ, when he raised him from the dead, and set him at his own right hand in the heavenly places, Far above all principality, and power, and might, and dominion, and every name that is named, not only in this world, but also in that which is to come: And hath put all things under his feet, and gave him to be the head over all things to the church, Which is his body, the fulness of him that filleth all in all. (Ephesians 1:17-23)*

**THE BELIEVER'S GUIDE TO THE APOSTOLIC MINISTRY** — A Comprehensive Study of the Apostolic Ministry in the Church

# -Book 5-
# The Constructing of the Apostolic Person:

## The Preparation of the Apostolic Person for Ministry and Service

Since all are not apostles, God makes the benefit of apostolic ministry available to all by placing an apostolic anointing on other members in the Body. In this book, we will examine individuals who possess an apostolic gift and grace.

The individual who possesses an apostolic anointing upon his/her life is referred to as an apostolic person. Apostolic people possess the same characteristics as apostles. They act as disciples, sons (or daughters), and big brothers (or sisters).

**THE BELIEVER'S GUIDE TO THE APOSTOLIC MINISTRY** — A Comprehensive Study of the Apostolic Ministry in the Church

# Introduction

Ministry and service in the kingdom of God is a privilege. God calls every member of the Body of Christ to serve for the benefit and welfare of the Body of Christ. However, we must remember that there are personal preparations that God requires for service.

The Potter's Wheel Study Series is designed to help believers recognize and apply the personal preparation that God implements for those called to minister and to serve.

It is our prayer that the minister and the laymen will respond to God's personal preparations for ministry and service.

**THE BELIEVER'S GUIDE TO THE APOSTOLIC MINISTRY** — A Comprehensive Study of the Apostolic Ministry in the Church

**THE BELIEVER'S GUIDE TO THE APOSTOLIC MINISTRY** — A Comprehensive Study of the Apostolic Ministry in the Church

## In this Publication

We learn from scriptures that the apostolic ministry was displayed first in the New Testament Church. Its role in the Church has been influential from the beginning. However, not everyone in the Church is an apostle. There is diversity in the Body of Christ.

> *Now ye are the body of Christ, and members in particular. And God hath set some in the church, first apostles, secondarily prophets, thirdly teachers, after that miracles, then gifts of healings, helps, governments, diversities of tongues. Are all apostles? are all prophets? are all teachers? are all workers of miracles? Have all the*

*gifts of healing? do all speak with tongues? do all interpret? But covet earnestly the best gifts: and yet shew I unto you a more excellent way. (I Corinthians 12:27-31 KJV)*

Since all are not apostles, God makes the benefit of apostolic ministry available to all by placing an apostolic anointing on other members in the Body. In this book, we will examine individuals who possess an apostolic gift and grace.

The individual who possesses an apostolic anointing upon his/her life is referred to as an apostolic person. Apostolic people possess the same characteristics as apostles. They act as disciples, sons (or daughters), and big brothers (or sisters).

**THE BELIEVER'S GUIDE TO THE APOSTOLIC MINISTRY** — A Comprehensive Study of the Apostolic Ministry in the Church

-Prologue-
# Understanding Anointings

**THE BELIEVER'S GUIDE TO THE APOSTOLIC MINISTRY** | A Comprehensive Study of the Apostolic Ministry in the Church

Today, believers worldwide have developed an appreciation for spiritual gifts and manifestations. However, misinterpretations of scripture have caused individuals to boast in possessing "anointings" that do not exist.

Before exploring the teaching anointing, we must develop a clear understanding of the anointing.

Both the Old and New Testaments contain numerous references to the anointing. The anointing is an important component in the service of the Lord. Under both covenants, the servants of the Lord could not serve without it.

The Hebrew and Greek terms for "to anoint" denote to smear or rub in. This implies that the anointing becomes a part of the individual who has received it.

## Anointings in the Old Testament

The scriptures tell us that there are diversities of anointings. This was true even under the Old Covenant.

The Hebrew term for anointing was mashchah (pronounced mash-khaw'). It means a consecratory gift and also to consecrate. This implies that the anointed individuals were gifts to those they ministered to.

In addition, they were set aside unto the purpose for which they were anointed.

In the Old Testaments texts, God anointed individuals to perform various tasks and stand in certain offices. They were anointed to stand in the offices of priest and king, through oil being poured upon them.

*Aaron anointed as a priest*

> *And thou shalt put them upon Aaron thy brother, and his sons with him; and shalt anoint them, and consecrate them, and sanctify them, that they may minister unto me in the priest's office. (Exodus 28: 41)*

*David anointed king by Samuel*

> *Then Samuel took the horn of oil, and anointed him in the midst of his brethren: and the Spirit of the Lord came upon David (I Samuel 16:13a)*

In each of these examples, the anointing of God was demonstrated by a physical anointing of the individual. However, others were anointed to stand in positions of authority without an outward anointing.

*The Judges*

> *Nevertheless the Lord raised up judges, which delivered them out of the hand of those that spoiled them. (Judges 2:16)*

*The Prophets*

> *Since the day that your fathers came forth out of the land of Egypt unto this day I have even sent unto you all my servants the prophets, daily rising up early and sending them. (Jeremiah 7:25)*

It is clear that God raised up the judges and prophets to stand in positions of great authority without an anointing ceremony. The Spirit of God anointed them. We discover that no one could function in any of the above offices except God placed them.

Though there were other individuals whom the Lord used, we find that God anointed individuals to stand as prophets, judges, priests, and kings continually.

In addition, there were other individuals anointed by God to function in other capacities without an anointing ceremony. Individuals such as the builders of the tabernacle, the seventy elders who prophesied after receiving Moses' spirit, Barak, Ezra, Nehemiah, Zerubbabel, and various others.

They received an anointing from God to accomplish specific tasks.

**Anointings in the New Testament**

After Christ's resurrection and the outpouring of the Spirit, we find that God still anointed individuals for service. We discover from the scriptures that men and women are anointed to stand in ministry offices such as apostles, prophets, evangelists, pastors, and teachers.

> *And he gave some, apostles; and some, prophets; and some, evangelists; and some, pastors and teachers. (Ephesians 4:11)*

Likewise, aside from functioning in ministry offices, individuals are anointed and endowed with certain gifts for Christian service. These other gifts and offices are listed in the book of I Corinthians and in the Book of Romans.

> *But the manifestation of the Spirit is given to every man to profit withal. For to one is given by the Spirit the word of wisdom; to another the word of knowledge by the same Spirit; To another faith by the same Spirit; to another the gifts of healing by the same Spirit; To another the working of miracles; to another prophecy; to another discerning of spirits; to another divers kinds of tongues; to another the interpretation of tongues. (I Corinthians 12:7-10)*

> *Having then gifts differing according to the grace that is given to us, whether prophecy, let us prophesy according to the proportion of faith; Or ministry, let us wait on our ministering: or he that teacheth, on teaching; Or he that exhorteth, on exhortation: he that giveth, let him do it with simplicity; he that ruleth, with diligence; he that sheweth mercy, with cheerfulness. (Romans 12:6-8)*

Though various terms are used in the New Testament to describe the anointing of the Spirit, two terms are seen frequently. The first is found in II Corinthians 2:21,

> *Now he which stablisheth us with you in Christ, and hath anointed us,*

*is God. (2 Corinthians 1:21 KJV)*

The Greek work for anointed in this text is chrio (pronounced khree'-o). It means to be consecrated to an office or religious service. Paul used this term to express that God had placed him in the apostolic office to minister to the Church.

Thus, we find that one receives an anointing to serve. If you are not called to a ministry office, there is an anointing on you to serve in some capacity. The second term used for anointing is found in I John 2:20,

> *But the anointing which ye have received of him abideth in you, and ye need not that any man teach you: but as the same anointing teacheth you of all things, and is truth, and is no lie,*

*and even as it hath taught you, ye shall abide in him. (I John 2:27 KJV)*

The Greek word used here is chrisma (pronounced khris'-mah). We derive the word charisma from this word. It is defined as the special endowment of the Holy Spirit. Hence, the anointing comes with gifts and endowments from God.

Therefore, as believers, we should consider the use of the expression, "I am anointed to do such and such" carefully. We must not confuse personal gifts and talents with the endowment of the Spirit.

When we receive the Spirit of God, its presence abides in us. The same is true for the anointing. When God places a particular anointing upon an individual, it remains. The gifts of God will operate according to the need and purpose of the moment.

However, the "anointings" or endowments of the Spirit abide with an individual at all times. Even in disobedience, the anointing to be king remained upon Saul. David recognized this (I Samuel 24:6).

**Office versus Anointing**

The Spirit of God governs all of the spiritual activities within the Body. He anoints and appoints according to the ultimate will of the Father.

Since the Body of Christ is made up of many members, there are various needs within it. The Spirit of God then anoints individuals to fulfill the needs within the

Body.

The greatest burden for ministry rests upon the leaders, specifically, the apostles, prophets, evangelists, pastors, and teachers. Their purpose is found in Ephesians 4:12:

1. 1.To perfect the saints
2. To train them for the work of the ministry
3. To build up the Church spiritually

However, these ministries are not responsible to minister to everyone. God uses the entire Body of Christ. The members of the Body of Christ are called to minister to one another, even if they are not called to a ministry office.

*As every man hath received the gift, even so minister the same one toward another, as good stewards over the manifold grace of God. (I Peter 4:10)*

Therefore, God anoints individuals to function in similar ways to those of the ministry offices.

Believers will have anointings on their lives, which, if not careful, may be mistaken for a call to a particular ministry office. This implies that there are some that have an apostolic gift without being called as an apostle.

Moreover, some have an anointing to prophesy without functioning in the office of the prophet. This is also true for teachers.

Numerous individuals today have laid claim to a teaching anointing without understanding all that they entail. Remember to never confuse a call to a ministry office with an anointing of the Holy Spirit. However, an individual with a apostolic anointing is identified as an apostolic disciple.

With this brief analysis of the anointing, we will now explore the teaching anointing and how God prepares one for this gift and ministry in the Church.

# -Chapter 1-
# Apostolic Person is a Disciple

**THE BELIEVER'S GUIDE TO THE APOSTOLIC MINISTRY** — A Comprehensive Study of the Apostolic Ministry in the Church

Apostolic people have a consuming passion and desire for Christ. They follow Christ daily. As the disciples left all to serve Christ, they will leave the world behind to please Him.

**Disciples of the Word**

Disciples are students and pupils. Apostolic people have a hunger and love for the things of God. They have a passion not only to learn of Him, but also to become as He is. The Word of God has priority in their lives.

**Disciples of the Loyalty**

Disciples follow their masters wholeheartedly. Apostolic people will follow Christ with all of their hearts. They have the ability to endure very trial and test in order to follow Him.

## Disciples of Discipline

Disciples are disciplined. Apostolic people will have a zeal for the holiness of God. Their lives will reflect the necessary discipline and self-control needed to remain in right standing with the Lord.

## Disciples of Christ's Example

Disciples have one goal: to become like their instructors. Apostolic people have a desire to be like Christ. Their goal is to reflect His image in their everyday lives. They have an undying urge to bring honor and glory to the Master.

## Disciples Respect Authority

Disciples respect their instructors. Apostolic people have respect for Christ and

His representatives. They will also respect leadership in the Church and in the government.

**THE BELIEVER'S GUIDE TO THE APOSTOLIC MINISTRY**  A Comprehensive Study of the Apostolic Ministry in the Church

**THE BELIEVER'S GUIDE TO THE APOSTOLIC MINISTRY**

A Comprehensive Study of the Apostolic Ministry in the Church

-Chapter 2-

# Apostolic Person is a Son (or Daughter)

**THE BELIEVER'S GUIDE TO THE APOSTOLIC MINISTRY**  A Comprehensive Study of the Apostolic Ministry in the Church

Ministry Guides Series

Apostolic people believe that God wants relationship above religion and sonship above service. They strive to be sons (and daughters) of God.

**Obedient**

Sons are obedient to their parents. Apostolic people will be true sons and daughters in ministry.

Even as Timothy was a son unto Paul, they will exemplify this in their relationships with Church leadership.

Not only will they be subject to leadership, but more importantly to the Word of God and the leading of His Spirit.

**Reflect**

Sons reflect the image of their fathers. Apostolic people endeavor to reflect the nature and character of Christ. They will be godly individuals reflecting the holiness of God. They follow the verse of scripture that states, "Be ye holy; for I am holy." (I Peter 1:16)

**Follow Example**

Sons follow the father's examples. Apostolic people believe that whatsoever things they have seen Christ do, they can do also. They will not only demonstrate the character and nature of God, but His works will follow them. They do not need a position or title, they believe because He said so. Apostolic people believe unquestionably in the following scriptures.

> *And these signs shall follow them that believe; In my name shall they cast out*

*devils; they shall speak with new tongues; (Mark 16:17)*

*They shall take up serpents; and if they drink any deadly thing, it shall not hurt them; they shall lay hands on the sick, and they shall recover. (Mark 16:18)*

*Verily, verily, I say unto you, He that believeth on me, the works that I do shall he do also; and greater works than these shall he do; because I go unto my Father. (I John 14:12)*

**THE BELIEVER'S GUIDE TO THE APOSTOLIC MINISTRY** — A Comprehensive Study of the Apostolic Ministry in the Church

-Chapter 3-
# The Apostolic Person is a Brother (or Sister)

The apostolic person believes in the family of the Church. They relate to other believers as if they were biological brothers and sisters. Their concern is genuine and heartfelt.

**Protect**

Big brothers protect their siblings. Apostolic people are watchful over their brothers and sisters in Christ. They will help immature and weak Christians in their walks. They believe that they are their brother's keeper. They will be sensitive to the needs of others through the Spirit of God.

**Godly Directives**

Big brothers enforce their parent's rules to their siblings. Apostolic people respect God and Church leadership. They will remind their brothers and sisters to follow the Word, the Spirit, and their leaders. They will endeavor to see others walk in obedience to Christ and leadership.

**Trustworthy**

Big brothers earn the trust of their parents. Apostolic people are respected by the leaders they serve under and by fellow believers.

Leaders will trust their advice and council because they do not seek to please themselves, but to please God and to serve leadership faithfully. Apostolic people will also have the respect of other members in the Body of Christ. This is due to the love and respect that they demonstrate towards Christ, leadership, and the brethren.

**THE BELIEVER'S GUIDE TO THE APOSTOLIC MINISTRY** — A Comprehensive Study of the Apostolic Ministry in the Church

-Chapter 4-

# The Apostolic Person's Character

**THE BELIEVER'S GUIDE TO THE APOSTOLIC MINISTRY**  A Comprehensive Study of the Apostolic Ministry in the Church

Because the apostolic person has the favor of God, the respect of leadership, and the support of the brethren, they must strive to reflect the nature of Christ at all times and resist pride. Paul gives the necessary character traits of which form the foundation of the character traits of apostolic people in his instructions to the Roman Church (Romans 12:9-17).

**Foundation of Love**

Apostolic people have to demonstrate genuine love. They must be lovers of good and despisers of evil in all forms. (Romans 12:9)

Apostolic people must love the brethren and seek the welfare of others above themselves. (Romans 12:10)

### Foundation of Faithfulness

Apostolic people have to resist procrastination and stagnation in ministry. They must maintain a zeal for the work of the Lord. (Romans 12:11)

Apostolic people have to be people of faith and prayer. They have to be able to endure tribulation, inspire hope in others and themselves, and be prayer warriors. (Romans 12:12)

### Foundation of Edification

Apostolic people have to be selfless. They must be willing to meet the needs of others and to be easily entreated. (Romans 12:13)

Apostolic people should speak words that edify and build up other believers at all times. They are not to be gossips and revilers. (Romans 12:14)

**Foundation of Community**

Apostolic people have to be in tune with other members of the Body. They, through the Spirit, have to be sensitive to the failures, trials, and successes of others. (Romans 12:15)

Apostolic people have to be impartial in their relationships with others. They should be as God who is no respecter of persons. (Romans 12:16)

Apostolic people have to be harmless. They ought to be gentle, representing the nature of God in all honesty. (Romans 12:17)

Anyone who feels he/she has an apostolic anointing has to guard themselves against pride, deception, and visions of greatness. In turn, they will be pillars in the midst of the Church.

# -Chapter 5-
# Recognizing the Apostolic Person

**THE BELIEVER'S GUIDE TO THE APOSTOLIC MINISTRY** — A Comprehensive Study of the Apostolic Ministry in the Church

The apostolic person will function uniquely in the Body of Christ. In order to recognize the apostolic person, one has to know the functions of apostolic individuals.

**Understanding of the Word**

Apostolic people carry the Word of God. Apostolic people understand and know how to make proper application of the scriptures.

They, like apostles, will understand many of the hidden things of God through scripture. They encourage other believers to study the Word of God.

*Study to shew thyself approved unto God, a workman that needeth not to be ashamed, rightly dividing the word of truth. But shun profane and vain babblings: for they will increase unto more ungodliness (II Timothy 2:15)*

## Understanding of Impartation

Apostolic people impart life into other believers. Apostolic people know how to communicate spiritual truths to help other believers grow in the knowledge of the Lord. Their words will consistently minister grace, wisdom, insight, hope, and faith to those around them.

*Let no corrupt communication proceed out of your mouth, but that which is good to the use of edifying, that it may minister grace unto the hearers. (Ephesians 4:29)*

## Understanding Development

Apostolic people help establish others

their walks with the Lord. Apostolic people have the spiritual insight to help babes and immature saints gain strength in the Lord. They will help them to overcome weaknesses and sins through wise counsel, prayer, and spiritual support.

> *Brethren, if a man be overtaken in a fault, ye which are spiritual, restore such an one in the spirit of meekness; considering thyself, lest thou also be tempted. Bear ye one another's burdens, and so fulfill the law of Christ. (Galatians 6:1-2)*

**Understanding Evangelism**

Apostolic people are shameless witnesses of the Lord. Apostolic people are gifted to evangelize in the name of the Lord.

Whether at home, at work, or out in public, they seek to win souls to the Kingdom of God.

They realize that their relationship with God, not a title, compels them to witness. They do this with great conviction and results.

> *But ye shall receive power, after that the Holy Ghost is come upon you: and ye shall be witnesses unto me both in Jerusalem, and in all Judaea, and in Samaria, and unto the uttermost part of the earth. (Acts 1:8)*

## Understanding Order

Apostolic people serve and support leadership. Apostolic people believe in divine order. They will support godly leadership without question. No matter what capacity they serve in the Church, it is done as unto the Lord and with respect unto God-given leadership. They also encourage others to follow the leadership as they follow the Lord.

> *Remember them which have the rule over you, who have spoken unto you the word of God: whose faith follow, considering the end of their conversation. (Hebrews 13:17)*

## Understanding Discernment

Apostolic people expose false doctrines and ministers. Apostolic people exercise mature discernment. They are zealous for the Lord and the purity of the Church. They have the wisdom to recognize false ministers and doctrines readily. They are bold in identifying the false while supporting the truth.

> *Beware of false prophets, which come to you in sheep's clothing, but inwardly they are ravening wolves. Ye shall know them by their fruits. Do men gather grapes of thorns, or figs of thistles? (Matthew 7:15-16)*

## Understanding Spiritual Gifts

Apostolic people possess the power and gifts of the Spirit. Apostolic people have the gifts in operation in their lives. They believe God in all things. They are believers who have powerful testimonies of the power of God being displayed in their everyday lives.

*And these signs shall follow them that believe; In my name shall they cast out devils; they shall speak with new tongues; They shall take up serpents; and if they drink any deadly thing, it shall not hurt them; they shall lay hands on the sick, and they shall recover. (Mark 16:17-18)*

Though apostolic people are scattered throughout the Body of Christ, no matter where they are, they bring life and stability among the congregation.

**THE BELIEVER'S GUIDE TO THE APOSTOLIC MINISTRY**  A Comprehensive Study of the Apostolic Ministry in the Church

-Chapter 6-

# Flourishing as an Apostolic Person

If you believe there is an apostolic anointing upon your life, there are certain practical steps to take to flow properly in it. Without these disciplines in your life, you will never flow fully in what God has for you.

**Flourish in Study**

Apostolic people have to consistently study and apply the Word of God to their lives. The Word has to rule their hearts and minds. The Word will equip them for service in the Body of Christ.

Apostolic people have to believe the scriptures are trustworthy. They must have faith that the Word is directly from God.

*All scripture is given by inspiration of God, and is profitable for doctrine, for*

> *reproof, for correction, for instruction in righteousness: That the man of God may be perfect, thoroughly furnished unto all good works. (II Timothy 3:16-17)*

**Flourish in Prayer**

Apostolic people have to be consistent in prayer. It is the only way to remain strong in the Lord. In addition, prayer will give them greater sensitivity in the Spirit.

Prayer will guide them to their rightful places in ministry. They should have a heart to pray also for local leadership that nothing hinders the spreading of the gospel.

> *Praying always with all prayer and supplication in the Spirit and watching thereunto with all*

*perseverance and supplication for all saints. (Ephesians 6:18)*

## Flourish in Submission

Apostolic people have to be submitted to local leadership. They must follow the vision of the leaders as they follow Christ. Without being submitted to authority, they will become ineffective in the Church.

*Remember them which have the rule over you, who have spoken unto you the word of God: whose faith follow, considering the end of their conversation. (Hebrews 13:7)*

**THE BELIEVER'S GUIDE TO THE APOSTOLIC MINISTRY** — A Comprehensive Study of the Apostolic Ministry in the Church

www.ingramcontent.com/pod-product-compliance
Lightning Source LLC
Chambersburg PA
CBHW050337010526
44119CB00049B/579